D1516238

**TAKE CARE**

**A Guide for Responsible Living**

# TAKE CARE

**L. David Brown**

**AUGSBURG** Publishing House • Minneapolis

TAKE CARE

*To my wife, Virginia,*
*the most refreshing caretaker I know*

# Contents

# Foreword

When David Brown came to our town, I had a few private doubts. I was certain that he would be a good preacher and was not disappointed. In fact, I came to look forward to his sermons, an unusual attitude for clergy consigned to pews.

I was less confident about his pastoral role. He had been a national executive in a specialized field—world hunger; would he have a genuine interest in the more ordinary affairs of life in rural Iowa? Earlier he had been a national youth director; how would he relate to other age groups?

My reservations were dispelled quickly. Dave and Virginia visited every home in the large congregation within ten months. It was soon apparent that he was not only interested in people as a category but in persons as individuals. He was and is concerned about conditions in Africa and Asia but he is fully committed to tasks within a few miles of home.

David Brown challenges and comforts people, rejoices and suffers with them. He cares. His broad experience makes him capable of speaking and writing on many subjects but because he cares, he is especially qualified to write this book.

Most of us are selective in our caring. We care for people we like and causes that interest us but neglect the unlovely and less interesting. Some among us are generous in support of missionaries to distant lands but reluctant to deal with the needs of persons in nearer neighborhoods. Others are active in congregational affairs but unconcerned about global matters. Still others are active in opposition to corporate injustice and oppression but capable of individual hostilities and cruelty. There are those whose giving through the church, according to David Preus, is characteristic of "spare change Christianity" and then there are the ones who give ostentatiously of their affluence while demonstrating a wasteful lifestyle which contrasts sharply with the unsatisfied needs of millions overseas.

The following chapters present a vision which goes beyond all these limited views of caring. Stewardship which is truly a response to God's grace involves all of life. Supporting the mission of the church is one special expression of stewardship and this, too, is comprehensive—embracing local, regional, national and global efforts, proclamation and service, education and advocacy. A faithful church will not be sporadic in its mission, generating support only in spurts, but will maintain and increase momentum on a continuing basis.

David Brown uses both long shots and close-ups in transmitting his vision. From global events and intimate observation of parish life, he selects scenes which are stimulating and revealing. He shares in the hope that others, too, will care.

JOHN W. BACHMAN

# Pre-word

"Take care. . . . " It almost seems to be displacing goodbye as a word of parting between friends. Good-bye is a contraction of the old English phrase, "God be with ye," which would make it an acceptable benediction for Christians, except for the fact that no one associates it with its original intent. And so, "take care" is an adequate replacement.

When we think about it, the expression conveys a double meaning. It is saying to another that he should care for himself and for everything for which he has responsibility. But it also expresses the desire that he should take care of *everything*. It also implies "give care."

Caring is a strong word. Some New Testament scholars think care might convey the meaning for the Greek word *agape* better than the word love. If we try it we will find it gives new meaning to a passage like 1 Corinthians 13.

Love is one of those badly misused words whose present-day meaning is a caricature of what it once expressed. We romanticize love to the point of trivializing it. Love is becoming a counterfeit word devoid of any redeeming social value. While it should be the most potent and virile word in a Christian's vocabulary, we dilute the Bible's meaning beyond recognition. Caring, on the other hand, somehow carries the freight of what we mean by loving the unlovable, or having concern for the powerless and oppressed.

Like love, *care* could be on the road to an accident mangling its meaning beyond recognition. It appears frequently in many magazine and TV ads. The tag line on the advertisements of one organization dedicated to assisting poor children around the world reads: "Thank you for caring enough!" As so many ads do, it takes off from the self-congratulatory slogan of a well-known greeting card company, "You cared enough to send the very best." Some ads speak of the care with which they make their product, while others stress the concern they have for you as a customer. I did business with a certain bank in Washington, D.C., until its newspaper ads started coming out with a big, bold, banner headline asking, "Who's going to care for you when you're old and gray?" As we listen to the radio or flip through a magazine we note how frequently the word care appears. Maybe that is a clue to its current power to convey meaning. The Madison Avenue hucksters know a good word when they use it.

This volume is about *taking care* of the bounty God

continually provides us. Taking care, also known as stewardship, may be described as the "management of life and resources in meeting the common needs of life and in fulfilling the mission of the Church" (Minutes, LWF Commission on Stewardship and Evangelism, August 11-16, 1968, Exhibit G, p. 2).

Caring may also be described as a Christian's "response-ability." God showers his good gifts on us, and even sends us his Holy Spirit who gives us the ability to repond.

At a particularly discouraging point in my life, a seasoned Christian gave me helpful advice. She said: "Dave, I have come to see there are only two kinds of people in the world—the takers and the givers. Those who take win some battles, but God knows the givers win the war." Pondering the statement in my somewhat depressed state led me to finally ask: "Has there ever been a more exciting time in which a Christian can live?" Maybe every Christian in every generation must come to that understanding. I now know I had come to believe that as I never had before.

This book, in a sense, is a response to that re-newed conviction. We will first seek to widen the horizons of the understanding of Christian mission in today's world. Jurgen Moltmann, the Christian theo-logian who has contributed so much to bringing the church back to its essential task in our time, writes in his book on the church:

> What we have to learn . . . is not that the church "has" a mission, but the very reverse: that the mis-sion of Christ creates its own church. Mission does

not come from the church; it is from mission and in
the light of mission that the Church has been understood *(The Church in the Power of the Spirit,*
p. 10).

Caretakers must always widen their perspective
on what the church's task is. And through that ex-
panding vision we would like to make life more
interesting by showing how by being caretakers we
can enhance personal life, health, family, and prop-
erty in the riches of the Gospel. The Christian church
today has many ministries, and they include the
sphere of social and political agencies that affect
our community, nation and world. We shall also ask
how a caretaker's life-style might affect their partici-
pation in the church's mission.

The ideas in this volume are designed to give perspective to life. I believe in the power of ideas. But
this book will not move readers to greater heights of
giving, unless, of course, the ideas contained herein
are attached to the explosive power of the Gospel
through the work of the Spirit.

Caretaking is a perspective on life. What goes on
about us day by day is not the only reality. The con-
sideration of where we came from and where we
are going and why we are here forges the stuff of
reality and gives momentum to our lives. Caretaking
allows the Christian to participate in the gathering
momentum for mission that Christ today is providing
in exciting ways for his people.

I acknowledge with deepest gratitude the great
help of Prof. Erna Moehl of Wartburg College, who
spent many hours wrestling with this manuscript,

giving it tender, loving care as only she can do. Also the counsel of Dr. John Bachman, Director of the Office of Communication and Mission Support of the American Lutheran Church, was invaluable in shaping the purpose and cast of this volume. I must also mention the long-suffering staff and members of the parish I serve, St. Paul's Lutheran Church of Waverly, Iowa, who criticized, typed and bore extra burdens while the manuscript was being developed. And as can be seen in the body of this volume, I am indebted to scores of caretakers who have touched my life with ideas, guidance, and stimulation.

*— David Brown*

# 1

# God Has Called Us to Care

> *Every one should remain in the state in which he was called* (1 Cor. 7:20).

After serving in a mission congregation, I accepted a call to serve in the national office of my church. I had enjoyed my work as a pastor, and soon found my ministry in the church offices equally satisfying.

We became acquainted with the man next door who managed a five and dime store. He had done well and had received several promotions. One night, enjoying a fall evening in his backyard, I happened to ask him how he liked his work.

"Dave, do you realize that almost every night I come home, head for the bathroom, and throw up? I can barely endure the things I must do." He had never even hinted at his dissatisfaction previously.

His comment set a whole series of wheels turning in my head. I was doing work I found fulfilling, and

in my self-centered way I had never considered
the possibility that a person could feel only disdain
toward his job. My experience with my neighbor led
me to ask that same question of hundreds of congregational members. I was troubled by the many who
expressed unhappiness about their work.

The results of my conversations prompted me to
read rather extensively about Luther's neglected concept of *vocatio* or "calling." The reformer's idea was
that each person, baptized into Christ and adopted
into the family of God, has a holy calling. Our occupation can be a part of the calling, and every occupation is as honorable before God as any other. If
we stop to think, we see that it is almost impossible
to name an occupation that is not honorable. However, beyond our occupational pursuits, our calling
includes many roles we perform in life, such as those
of parent, child, citizen, friend, volunteer, spouse,
church or club members and many others that might
more particularly apply to different people's lives.
Some people find their calling best fulfilled in an
avocation or in the hours spent giving themselves to
a project that does not bring remuneration. The calling of others seems to be that of being friends to
scores of other human beings. One person I knew as
a boy who had a somewhat grubby, nondescript
job, my father called a "walking hymn of praise,"
because he continually befriended people in need.

Luther also made a point of saying that we do not
do our daily work "to the glory of God," but simply
as a service to other human beings. He did not want
anyone tempted to turn their daily work into "works"

that might become merit badges for salvation. Therefore all Christians are "full-time Christian servants,"
and not just those professionally employed by the
church. One of my pastoral colleagues never tires of
reminding our congregational members that "we
have 2600 ministers of Christ in St. Paul's Lutheran
Church."

My original conversation with my occupationally
unhappy neighbor led to many more. We probed
together what was wrong and why he did not like
his work. His attitudes revealed that he had no
understanding that his management was a way of
serving people. He saw no connection between
changing price tags, ordering Halloween masks, rearranging merchandise, and correcting salespersons
as an expression of his calling from God. "Why, I
never thought about my work as having any relationship to my faith," he confessed after we had had
several good talks about "calling." In other words,
his attitude to his job had precluded it as a way of
serving and caring. Later he was to change positions and to find much greater fulfillment in his new
work. Was it the change in jobs or a change in attitude that made a difference? He could never quite
say.

A recent Gallup Poll indicates that well over half
of the American working population are dissatisfied
with their jobs. Even after a casual reading of Studs
Terkel's insightful book, *Working*, I am struck by
how many people do not like what they are doing.
In the introduction, which is worth the price of the
book, Terkel comments:

Perhaps it is this specter that most haunts working men and women: the planned obsolescence of
people that is of a piece with the planned obsolescence of the things they make. Or sell. It is perhaps this fear of no longer being needed in a world
of needless things that most clearly spells out the
unnaturalness, the surreality of much that is called
work today *(Working,* p. xxii).

We would have to be hopeless romantics to contend that all people everywhere can have a clear
sense of God's calling in what they do. If we would
try to tell the fellow in the packing plant who does
nothing all day except cut off pigs' tails that his
work should be fulfilling he would be likely to take
a poke at us.

Terkel disabuses us of many of the sentimental notions we attribute to certain jobs. Through a young
cabbie he reminds the journalist who makes every
cabdriver a philosopher that most drivers will agree
with almost anything their passenger says, no matter
how absurd, as they are angling for a tip. Terkel sum-
marized the frustrations of an assembly line worker
in a steel plant: "It isn't that the average working guy
is dumb. He's tired, that's all." The worker adds
rhetorically, "Who you gonna sock? You can't sock
General Motors . . . you can't sock the system." "So,"
Terkel adds, "at the neighborhood tavern he socks
the patron sitting next to him, the average working
guy" (p. xxvii).

Because of the gargantuan technology we created through the use of mass production, many
observers believe Luther's concept of vocation just
does not fit anymore. My querying of a large num-

ber of laypersons about their work would concur with that evaluation, except for one thing. As Terkel points out there are scores of people who might not find any satisfaction in their job, but who nevertheless have a zest for life and are being fulfilled. The key is found in that little word *care*. Almost any job we can mention offers opportunities for being a caretaker. Caring has to do primarily with people. It might also have something to do with assembly lines and technology, but above all else caretaking is relational. The persons I find to be ministering in their work are the ones who have found ways to demonstrate their Christian concern to other workers, customers, and whoever else they may come into contact with in their daily tasks.

William Diehl, in his thoughtful book *Christianity and Real Life,* gives a striking illustration of how we separate our faith from the world in which we work. He tells about Earnest Seal, an early retiree from a supervisor's job in a steel company, who took a custodian's job in a large Baltimore church. He was tired of working with people who did not care about their work or about the quality of their product. In his janitorial duties he could work alone and would not have to hassle uncaring subordinates. He once told Diehl, "I remember what Paul said, that 'whatever you do, do it for the glory of God!' I suppose he was speaking about Christianity, but I think it can apply in real life as well" (p. 22).

Now we might argue that Seal's interpretation of Paul is faulty, but that is irrelevant to the point Diehl makes. He says the church failed to serve Earnest

Seal. If he could believe that there was a separation between Christianity and "real life," the church had missed an opportunity with this man somewhere along the line. Keeping in mind the distinction Luther insisted on as to serving our fellows in our work, we would have to say that there is a group of workers worse off because Seal left his former job. The church made him a custodian, but not a caretaker.

Luther's advice, based on his interpretation of the verse at the beginning of this chapter, was that Christians should remain in their present occupation. Gustaf Wingren quotes a portion of Luther and then goes on to point out how Luther views this chapter's opening passage:

> On earth actions vary in glory and importance. "But the eyes of God regard not works but our obedience in them. Therefore it is his will that we also have regard for his command and vocation." In this connection Luther, as usual, refers to I Corinthians 7:20. By giving heed to the duties imposed by one's vocation a person becomes a useful member of the whole body. Its different members serve different functions; but its unity and co-ordination are not disrupted because of this (*Luther on Vocation*, p. 178).

The central point Luther sought to make about our daily work is that we must do it well, as though we *cared*, and in that way serve other human beings. We therefore can serve others just as well in so-called secular jobs as in the professional positions in the church. This understanding has some implications for the way laypersons participate in the life of their parish. It is not difficult to imagine how the business of the parish would hum if members equipped with a myriad of skills and abilities felt free to offer their talents. However, when we place a highly skilled manager of a large plant on the trustees, it seems as though he left his resources at his desk. His aptitude for planning, expediting, managing and dreaming seem to evaporate. Or if some committee does give birth to an idea that makes eminently good sense, everybody feels constrained to wait until it can be checked out by the pastor. We might call this the "nontransferable talents syndrome." It is deeply rooted in the life of every parish I have served or in which I have held membership. In some cases it may be the pastor's fault, but I have seen this syndrome persist when the pastor did everything possible to eradicate it.

We do not mean to imply by the above that the lay minister's talents are mainly aimed at the parish. The crucial place for ministry is in the life of the world and, more particularly, in the occupation to which that person is called. I have often thought we should have commissioning services for the various occupations represented in a congregation's membership. And if people become so busy in their tasks "out there" that they can not help much in the parish, we should bless them and thank them all the more.

However, we can take our call to care so seriously that only our repeated failures loom before us. The Good News is that it is finally God who truly cares. He demonstrated what caring is in the cross. He cares through us, only as his forgiveness is renewed daily in us.

There are millions of unemployed and underemployed people in our world. Increasing rapidly are the number of retired people in our society, many of whom are at the prime of their ability to serve. Can we release these people to see that they, too, "remain in the state in which they are called"?

Lutheran General Hospital in Chicago strategically utilizes 700 persons as a volunteer force. From a civil engineer who is retired and now delivers papers to the patients to a busy housewife who gives two mornings a week in the emergency room, they demonstrate that if given a chance they have a big capacity for caring. Dubbing himself the "paper boy," the engineer seeks to make eye contact and bring a greeting to every bed to which he delivers a paper. The housewife knows people are especially frightened in the emergency ward and that the medics are far too busy to give much of a personal touch so she may be found holding a restless child for a doctor, taking a patient for X rays or keeping a patient's family informed of treatment being given. The Gospel has a wide-angle lens that reveals to us a caring that is people-centered and not task-oriented.

God's forgiving care flows out of Baptism. It seals the truth that we are part of a pilgrim people journeying through a sin-drenched world. At the font we are invited into the world to perform the roles God ordained for us. To begin with, our task is to be children and students. Our duties could develop someday to those of parents or spouses. Whether they do or not is not of importance because whatever our role, it is guaranteed by our Baptism. From that point on, God mysteriously leads us step-by-step into those roles he wishes us to shoulder.

The whelming goodness of Baptism does not mean it is given without pain. Dr. William Streng of Wartburg Seminary says that one of the best sermons on Baptism he ever heard was given in the midst of a proclamation in which the pastor addressed the parents of a child to be baptized that morning. The preacher asked: "Are you willing to accept the pain this child may experience through this act? Should the child in its lifetime live under an authoritarian rule and be denied the privilege of education, a decent job or having children, will you accept that responsibility?" Dr. Streng thought that couple walked rather slowly to the font that day.

God's grace does not promise us an earthly walk devoid of danger and risk. It is a calling to every believer to join the others so cleansed in a walk rife with scorn, tribulation and possibly even persecution. It is not magic, but a mystery. Part of that mystery is the calling into a none-too-perfect world. While we are led into that mystery with a deep and abiding joy in our hearts, we are beckoned into the realities of the world as it is. We are called to care, but our caring is not only for heavenly mysteries but for the earthly ones as well.

Recently, Bishop Manas Buthelezi of the Central Diocese of the Evangelical Lutheran Church in Southern Africa spoke to our congregation. He is known throughout the world for his courageous, nonviolent stand against the Republic of South Africa's policies of racial discrimination. He did not dwell upon the atrocities committed in that troubled land, but graphically portrayed the tremendous odds faced by the blacks in their struggle for justice. He had, for a time, been banned by the government; however, because of the enormous outcry of world public opinion, the government took the unusual step of lifting the ban. Almost anyone who seeks to do something about that situation is considered to be, not a Christian, but a communist sympathizer. That was the charge leveled against him. Did he have hope? He spoke of a "lonely hope" carried in his heart because of the crucifixion and resurrection of his Lord. We are invited to stand in solidarity with those who bear the suffering of "lonely hope." Dr. Buthelezi indicated that it was not liberal Christians who had provided genuine help, but members of the Jewish community of Johannesburg who went on the line for black brothers and sisters giving up their businesses and professional practices to do so.

Christ's calling is to care. Caring can be manifest in our jobs, with our families, through volunteer work and in a number of other ways. In our kind of world the Christian is called to reach out and identify with those whose daily vocation is one of suffering and oppression, propelled into their appointed tasks only by means of a "lonely hope."

# 2

# Undivided Caring

*Therefore I tell you do not be anxious about your life* (Matt. 6:25).

Some twenty years ago a group of people employed in youth ministries of the Lutheran church were discussing what they felt to be the single most important misunderstanding that young people in that day carried with them in regard to the faith. After considerable debate it was agreed that many of our youth possessed a "half-Gospel" faith. They accepted the deity of Christ, but had trouble with regard to his true humanity. There was a tendency to spiritualize everything. What was spiritual was good, but that which was material was somehow evil. They even seemed to conceive of their personhood in such a fashion. God, after all, was interested only in the soul because the body was the center of corrupt desire. As Swinburne had warned, they were "serving up half a Christ."

We decided some literature and program material was needed in this area because such a skewing of the faith could lead finally to despair. One thing that was decided upon was a series of short booklets on various phases of this subject. We pondered what the series might be titled when it struck me that the "Fulness Series" might be an apt name. And so there were born a number of brief volumes designed to address this topic. I still see them on library shelves and in pastors' studies. The books moved well, which told us that this was an area we needed to address.

In this connection, it might be helpful for us to pay greater attention to the use of the word *fulness* in the New Testament. Paul utilizes this word in speaking of the integrity of Christ and his people. The Apostle sprinkles that word throughout the book of Colossians as it applies to Jesus such as in 2:9, ". . . in him the whole fulness of deity dwells bodily." And so we confess in our creeds that he is "true God" and "he became *man*." In Ephesians the word extends to apply also to God's people. Our liaison with Christ continues day by day "until we all attain to the unity of the faith, and of the knowledge of the Son of God, to mature manhood, to the measure of the stature of the fulness of Christ" (4:13).

Even as we cannot emphasize the divinity of Jesus and neglect his humanity, so we should not exalt spiritual things and denigrate the material. Jesus deliberately combined earthly elements with the word of God in instituting the sacraments. They were the most common and simple elements in the households of his day. He perhaps could have established the sacraments by the laying on of hands, or by making the sign of the cross. But no, he chose water, wine, and bread. Though we use these earthly elements sparingly, that should not diminish their importance in partaking of the sacraments. Perhaps the fact that most Christians practice sprinkling in Baptism and ingest a thin wafer and thimbleful of wine should remind us that we do not have unlimited resources in the earth; and, indeed, there are millions that have not enough of these elements to sustain daily life. The Bible can speak of the sacramental acts as an inundation of cleansing power and a feast of glorious assurance because the word takes these tiny elements and multiplies their graciousness to us. The sacraments remind us that we are caretakers of the earth and of the material.

Another dualism we tend to create in the church is that of body and soul. When we ignore the wonders of the body, is it surprising that young people have a hard time seeing the superb beauty of human sexuality? Perhaps if we stressed that the body is the "temple of the Holy Spirit," the care of our health would be more than an occasional fad. We need both bodily and spiritual exercising. Not too many give up morning prayers for jogging, but it would be a pity if anyone gave up either. We need to eat right to protect these wondrous machines God has given us as well as practice prayer and meditation. Some doctors claim that as much as 75 percent of today's diseases are psychosomatic, that is, the body's illness is related to matters of the mind and spirit. And should we not be done with language that speaks of "saving souls"? Scholars agree that God, in both Testaments, addresses the *whole* person. God converts persons, not disembodied spirits.

Now the tendency to create what I call psychological dualism of such things as the personhood of Jesus Christ, or the material vis-a-vis the spiritual, or the separation of body and soul has its implications for the mission of the church. We have been troubled in the American church since the twenties with the difference between those supporting evangelicalism and those espousing a social gospel. The question often comes down to whether or not we can feed and clothe poverty-stricken people before we preach the Good News to them. The Lutherans took on an interesting debate following World War II. The Americans wanted to assist the war-ravaged brothers and sisters in Europe by providing housing, food, and clothing. In its most simplistic form the question was: Shall we not send them Bibles prior to sending the physical necessities? Thank God, the debate did not last long. We sent what they needed as persons.

But also today the same issue rages. Should we not first preach Good News to the millions living in poverty in the so-called "third" and "fourth" worlds of Asia, Latin America, and Africa? (The designations of third and fourth world are contrasted with the so-called first and second worlds dominated by the U.S. and the U.S.S.R.) Can we say to the undernourished of the world: "Go and be warmed"? Our Lord could not do that. The Gospel has a wide-angle lens that addresses the whole person in his need, whether that be physical or spiritual. In this present time before God establishes his new heaven and new earth, we cannot afford to be so heavenly minded as to be no earthly good. Christianity has been called the most materialistic religion in the world. We need not let our evangelistic task suffer in our goal to provide material necessities through such agencies as Catholic Relief Services, Church World Service, and Lutheran World Relief.

Our attitude toward mission is changing and especially among the young. There is a fast-growing group of young evangelicals who incorporate a radical social gospel with the radical decisiveness of being born again in Jesus Christ. Several magazines such as *Sojourners* and *The Other Side* illustrate this fusing of concern about both the body and the soul of the poor. Richard Quebedeaux has written an enlightening little paperback on this phenomenon.

> The New Evangelicals are, in fact, displaying a fresh interest in the social dimension of the Gospel. Their emphasis is still on spiritual rebirth, but a strong effect is being made to relate the inward change of heart to the demands of a more righteous society. For them, individual conversion is the precondition for revolutionary social transformation, yet conversion *by itself* is not enough to bring about such change. It must be supplemented by a practical social involvement together with all men and women of good will *(The Young Evangelicals, p. 38).*

In fact, a clearer understanding of this wholeness of God's concern for both body and spirit may be emerging among the so-called "evangelical community" to a greater extent than in mainline churches. The International Congress on World Evangelization drew up a remarkable covenant in their conference in Lausanne in 1974 in which there is both confession and renewed desire to attend the needs of the poor.

> . . . we express penitence both for our neglect and for having sometimes regarded evangelism and social concern as mutually exclusive. Although reconciliation with man is not reconciliation with God, nor is social action evangelism, nor is political liberation salvation, nevertheless we affirm that evangelism and socio-political involvement are both part of our Christian duty. For both are necessary expressions of our doctrines of God and man, our love for our neighbor and our obedience to Jesus Christ. The message of salvation implies also a message of judgment upon every form of alienation, oppression and discrimination, and we should not be afraid to renounce evil and injustice wherever they exist.

A remarkable example of wholeness in mission endeavor is being crafted by missionary David Simonson in Tanzania. First of all, he has identified closely with the people he serves. He continually speaks of their dignity and worth. He also respects what the struggling government of President Julius Nyerere is seeking to do. The Tanzanian government with great perception undertakes as its first priority building what we might call "middle schools." Simonson, a builder with both material and spiritual talents, travels far and wide in northern Tanzania to show various village people how they might use indigenous materials to construct schools according to government standards. He spends a minimum amount of time in showing how to start such projects, and checks on construction only occasionally, placing his confidence in the villagers' considerable abilities. When the building is erected and inspected, the government almost immediately sends out a well-trained teacher. This teacher is not only equipped to give the children of the village a well-rounded education, which includes a study of low-level agricultural technology, but offers courses in literacy for the adults of the village. In addition, the teacher has the children construct an experimental farming plot near the village for demonstration purposes. The spin-off effects are almost endless. The fathers and mothers build the school. Simonson only provides some behind-the-scenes tips on building. Meanwhile he continually prompts his friends in America, through an agency known as Operation Bootstrap-Tanzania, to send money for those materials that can not be constructed by the villagers. A small investment of time and money by caretaker Simonson and caretakers in this country pays off in a few years with new agricultural inputs, higher protein diets, a yearning for greater knowledge and economic growth. Hope results.

Next, the natives are asking what it is that causes Simonson to give so much of himself in such a self-effacing manner. They ask him, in short, to come and tell the Gospel story. This is one of the fastest growing mission areas in the world. Simonson cannot divide his concern. He cares about the Tanzanians as people. He does not choose to violate their personhood by asking them to hear the Gospel before he aids them in building their school. The Holy Spirit is using this new style of mission all over the world.

In my work as Executive Director of the American Freedom from Hunger Foundation, I had occasion to review over six hundred self-help development programs. The most effective ones are being carried out by Christians with a new understanding of an undivided mission. Many development experts who have no interest in the church agree with that assessment. We need not be on the defensive in the church in this regard. Many of our missionaries and those who work for Lutheran World Relief are creatively building models of self-help programs that are being emulated in many other places.

We cannot divide caring. The caretaker enfolds both the material tools God has given us to use as well as the spiritual needs of people to accomplish his mission. When we embrace the material things of the earth warmly, our spirituality deepens. If we look upon the body as something fearfully and wonderfully made, we will probe new depths of our souls. When God sent Jesus as his incarnate Son, he told us in a powerful way that our caring can not be divided.

# 3

# Caring Solo
# and in Formation

> *But you are a chosen race, a*
> *royal priesthood, a holy nation,*
> *God's own people* . . . (1 Peter
> 2:9).

We often hear people declare, "One solitary person
cannot make a difference in our complicated world."
Yet because the tentacles of mass communication
reach into every hamlet and city, every home and
ranch in this nation, and increasingly into the world,
that statement just is not true anymore. One thinks
of Rosa Parks, a black woman who would not be
content with sitting in the back of the bus in Mont-
gomery, Alabama, and was arrested December 1,
1955, and thereby began a civil rights revolution that
is not over yet.

The churches of my community asked people to
respond to a call by the organization known as Bread
for the World, a Christian lobbying movement in

support of the hungry of the world, to write their
congressman in support of the "Right to Food" resolution being considered by the Congress in 1975.
Over three hundred letters were mailed from our
small, rural community to a congressman who was
originally against the bill. Most of these people had
never written their congressman previously. What
resulted was that this man was instrumental in getting that resolution out of the Agricultural Committee, of which he was a member, and made a stir-
ring speech in support of the right of all people to
have enough to eat. The resolution passed, and the
Executive Director of Bread for the World, Arthur
Simon, told me later that that was an extremely important factor in having this action taken. Sometimes the only way we can show that we care is by
an individual acting in a personal way on behalf of
someone's need. But it is also true that there are
many things that can be accomplished only as we
act in concert.

We act in personal response to need because of a
personal encounter with Christ. We confess a personal God who reaches down into our personal center
to touch us with his grace. For the Christian, God is
not an abstraction. He is as personal as Jesus Christ.
God is made clear in his revelation through Jesus
Christ, and we do not need to rely on what we can
dimly perceive in the order and fitness of nature.
God identifies with our personal tragedies and with
our rising and falling moods and feelings. Jesus was
tempted in all things, as we are. From him, we learn
to care on a one-to-one basis. Jesus also shows us the

fitness of group action. He chose twelve who later "turned the world upside down" and established the corporate body of his church. When he fed the thousands, he had his disciples organize them into manageable groups and proceeded by that means to feed them all. There are certain things for which only corporate action can get the task of caring accomplished.

The sacraments embody both a personal and corporate concern by our Lord. Baptism is an intensely personal matter. We say that in Baptism the individual is named by Jesus and is washed in the forgiveness his cross made possible. But what else happens in that act? The child or adult is adopted into the family of God, the communion of saints. We have done grievous damage to the corporate aspect of Baptism by permitting this gift to be given in the privacy of a home or in an empty church with only family and sponsors present. The Danes have a tradition that assumes the entire congregation serves as sponsors for the person being baptized. That may be impractical in our mobile society, but the idea certainly symbolizes that a life has now become a part of the community.

And thus it is with Holy Communion. Many times we walk to the altar with a hunger and a thirst for the righteousness that only his body and blood can assuage. We are convicted by the guilt of our personal sin, and we desperately need this tangible expression of God's favor for our own person. Perhaps too seldom do we give thought to the fact that this sacrament also is an act of communion with one another as well as with Christ. It is not an act toward the person without also being an act of the community. Is that not the force of Jesus' admonition to go and be reconciled to our brother and sister *before* bringing our gift to the altar? In the case of the sacrament, God brings the gift to us *so that* we can bring the gift of reconciliation to others. We all have known older saints who would move mountains before they would give up receiving the sacrament in their home church with fellow believers. Many must move the mountains of arthritic pain, crippled appendages, or sluggish muscles to do so. Some parishes have the deacons take bread and wine from the altar to bring to the homes of shut-ins as a part of their weekly celebration of the sacrament. Whether that practice is followed or not, we consider "private communion" to be a corporate act, even as we use only first person plural pronouns when praying the Lord's Prayer.

The dual nature of the church made up of individuals that form a whole can be seen in the pictures the Bible draws describing the communion of saints. There are precious few definitions in the Bible. Its language is in the form of images and portraits, and especially is this true as we reflect on the scriptural portrayal of what the church is and does. There are many of these pictures of the church, such as head-body (Eph. 4:15-16); vine-branches (John 15:1-8); shepherd-sheep (John 10:1-18); cornerstone-bricks (Eph. 2:20); bride-groom (John 3:29); and the like. These pictures do not give us a precise definition of the church. From them we know that the lifeblood comes from him who is the head, vine, shepherd, cornerstone, and groom. The church is nothing without the thought, vitality, concern, strength, and love of Jesus.

These pictures of the church tell us that we are individually related to Jesus Christ. Each of us represents different parts of the body depending on our function and talents. Each branch has been grafted to the vine at the cost of Christ's blood. Each individual sheep is so important that the shepherd "leaves the ninety-nine to go after the one that is lost." The pictures of the church in the New Testament never relinquish the idea that each believer is special in the eyes of God. In fact, our individual differences are celebrated as in the image of the body. "If the foot were to say, I am not a hand, and so I do not belong to the body, would that mean that it stopped being part of the body?" (1 Cor. 12:15).

Yet the individual diversity creates the unity of the church. It is only in our differences that we can come together and function effectively. Paul says that the church is sustained in her life of mission by reaching out to draw into her membership the most diverse people to be found. That is the strange paradox of the Gospel, i.e., the differences we have between us are the measure of our unity, and this unity gives us greater effectiveness in accomplishing the purpose of the body. There are some functions of caring in which we can only act alone, but it is equally true that there are many tasks that can only be done by acting together. When we are called to care together, we need to celebrate our diversity as that is what will make our care count. These biblical pictures are all the more striking when we consider how many human institutions depend on the homogeneity of their members for accomplishing their goals.

There are dangers when the mission of Christ flies only in solo. Satan's supreme victory occurs within an individual when faith crosses over the line from being personal to being self-centered. If a personal testimony boasts of *my* encounter with Christ and disqualifies others who have not had my unique experience, then the devil has turned that relationship inward to a self-centered and self-serving faith. When "my God and I walk through the fields together," we may not be walking on God's turf at all. I recently heard a young man who searches for runaway youngsters speak about his experience in sharing Christ with these lost young people. "We introduce them to Jesus, and they have what I call a 'milk faith,' but we work very hard soon to get them into a Christian church where they can experience a 'meat faith'; otherwise, their 'milk faith' almost always shrivels up and dies."

While there are dangers in the stress on the personal, there are perils in an exclusive concern for the body politic also. My wife must remind me every so often that my grand concern for humanity, and especially the world's hungry, does not excuse me from taking time to be with my family. The celebrated Hartford Declaration by a group of theologians deeply involved in the social activism of the sixties stated that social concern can easily atrophy unless it is fueled by a person's continual worship of a transcendent and personal God.

Anthropologists tell us that there are two basic value systems. One is of the Western variety whose mark is competition and whose end is glorifying individual achievements. The other, found in older cultures of Africa, Asia, and Latin America, is cooperative in nature. This should not be viewed in some romantic fashion as if the cooperation consists only of a spirit of brotherly-sisterly love. Rather cooperation in these economies of scarcity is a plain necessity. If our only hope of survival is the assistance of a neighbor or tribal member, then we learn through bitter experience to cooperate. We should not make easy judgments about which value system, the competitive or the cooperative, is the better one. They are different, but the difference can be instructive.

It is my observation that the appreciation for the corporate in church life is stronger in the so-called "young churches" in the older cultures of the Third World than in the West. I see a deep sense of gratitude permeating the Christians in Africa. They are grateful for the gift of Jesus Christ, and their relationships are often marked by continuous outpourings of gratitude to one another. They have a deep sense of gratitude for their brothers and sisters in Christ around the globe as well. They cannot seem to say thank you enough. They know what it is to be dependent on each other, even as their dependency on Western churches diminishes. God is using their cultural rearing in a cooperative structure to give their witness a sense of the corporateness of the church. On the other hand, African Christians do not de-emphasize the personal in their faith. They only enhance it with a strong sense of community, local and worldwide.

An Air Force pilot who flies in a crack group of formation fliers told me not long ago that "anyone who becomes even slightly individualistic or who is not exactly in the place he is supposed to be will cause me to pull out of the formation altogether." He does that periodically whether they are being viewed by no one, as in practice, or watched by thousands. He took up that dangerous work because he enjoys it as much as flying solo, if not more. He loves developing the intricate skills formation flying demands. With him, however, one never comes to know too much, and one always respects every other pilot in that formation. Such flying calls for constant vigilance and continual cooperation.

The church flies in some pretty dangerous skies. It often cannot survive going solo. It is my view that we American Christians must wrestle harder with what it means to fly in formation. We do not do that at the expense of sacrificing a personal faith or individual concern. Recently, Billy Graham took his crusade behind the Iron Curtain into Hungary. While he was there, it was reported that he said he would no longer find it so easy to preach about "godless communism." He explained upon his return to this country that Christians can live in any economic system, and that he was grateful that there were Christians living behind the Iron Curtain. If that be his conviction, it is another example of an expanded heart. It is on a par with his dramatic decision after returning from Africa that he would no longer preach to segregated audiences. It is a tribute to this influential man that he can cast away narrowness and publicly embrace a broader vision. When flying in formation in the church, we may find ourselves next to some strange aircraft and sometimes in foreign skies!

Caring, in our day, requires that we often must be involved in intricate social, economic, and political issues. Some contend the church must stay out of politics, especially if the issue does not correspond with their own personal views. Surely the message of the Scriptures is that God wants his servants to fight injustice foisted upon people because of racism, sexism, or economic oppression. That cannot be done without Christians being informed about these issues and joining in concerted action to correct abuses. The issues are not always crystal clear, but I firmly believe they are becoming clearer.

The decision about the "Right to Food" legislation could not have come to pass without political involvement by many caring Christians. Indeed there is no way that the plight of starving people in the southern hemisphere will be rectified unless there are massive changes in the priorities of our government. Churches and voluntary agencies cannot accomplish the task alone, as important as it is for us to continue to extend our support of them.

A pastor from South Korea, Kim Mong Eun, has put the case well for flying in formation also in political skies.

Passing moral judgments on political, economic, or social matters is one of the duties of the church. Such moral judgments are one of the most effec-

tive ways of cooperation the church may offer to
the state, because in any human society there are
always faults which need to be cured. Christians
have their own outlook on life, on society, and on
the whole universe. They believe that God has his
own plan for humankind, and they believe that they
have to cooperate with God in carrying out that
project. If they fail to cooperate, they do not deserve to be called Christians. A non-prophetic
Christian church is nonsense.

These are strong words, and they call the caring
church to be a prophetic voice. Sometimes that voice
may be singing solo, as in the case of Rosa Parks.
More generally, we in the American church must
struggle to raise our caring voices in concert, so that
we may be heard also in the halls of Congress and
within the walls of state legislatures.

# 4

# Culture Caring

> *But a Samaritan . . . when he*
> *saw him, he had compassion*
> (Luke 10:33).

One of my former professors at the University of Minnesota offered me an exciting opportunity to join him in a research study he was just beginning in the field of intercultural communication. He now has a wide reputation and is highly sought after by multinational corporations because customs and practices can have such opposite meanings in different parts of the world. Businessmen have learned that whether in their personal contact or in advertising campaigns, certain things done in this country can be very offensive to people of different cultural backgrounds. For example, we are used to standing up as a sign of respect. In countries of the Far East where the custom requires that one should look up to a person of elevated rank, the sign of respect is to sit down. The differences are legion and the value of knowing

45

about those differences is not exclusive to the business world, but is a matter of serious study by the diplomatic corps, educators, foreign aid experts, missionaries and anyone who travels widely or resides in a different country. Cross-cultural studies are becoming very important in our interdependent world. I have since resumed contact with Dr. Howell and am even more fascinated by his field of study because it has become such a needed and sought-after discipline.

We spoke in the last chapter about Paul's insistence that the unity of the church depends on its diversity. That means that the Christian becomes sensitive to the wide differences, not only among individuals, but also among cultures. That is what we may call culture caring.

Caring for people who are like us is certainly the easiest. The Fuller School of Theology has been speaking for a number of years about "homogenized evangelism," which means that Christians of like background can the more easily reach people of similar background. Some say that in establishing American mission congregations or in the general field of evangelistic work persons from a northern European heritage should concentrate on areas where people of that background live. This has been a chief characteristic of Lutheran mission policy in this country. It makes sense. However, others have been raising questions about this approach, taking a cue from Paul's understanding of the church as a body that defines its unity in its diversity. Can we ignore the inner city, or reaching out with our universal Gospel to people of differing ethnic origins?

We say of our country that it is a melting pot. This nation welcomed people from many nations and situations. The great lady in New York Harbor beckons all with a taste for freedom:

> . . . Give me your tired, your poor,
> Your huddled masses yearning to breathe free,
> The wretched refuse of your teeming shore.
> Send these, the homeless, tempest-tost to me,
> I lift my lamp beside the golden door!

This dimension of the great experiment this country became is one of the most exciting in the history of nation-states. When we consider the pluralism represented by immigrants from eastern, southern, and northern Europe as well as from the British Isles, it is easy to apply the melting pot appellation. When we spice this mixture with large influxes from Africa and the Caribbean, diversity multiplies. No nation has invited in such large numbers peoples of different economic, cultural, national and social lines. Some who were not invited, but coerced, have contributed an astonishing richness to our cultural heritage.

However, the celebration of this diversity has been receding. We tended to make our multicultural stew look like something run through a blender. We have sometimes expected people to act and talk in a certain way if they were going to be called "American." In this century there began the flight to the suburbs, and the homogenization became more pronounced. Perhaps that trend is being reversed by the new appreciation of our different ethnic groups. It should be fervently hoped that a new "Declaration of Independence" is being written that will apply to all peoples within our borders.

There is evidence that white Christians are continuing to awaken to the rich heritage of the black churches and peoples. Toynbee says that the only indigenous religious music produced in the United States of any note is the black spiritual. These quietly simple but profound hymns bespeak a deep joy born out of the pathos of slavery. Some of our finest Christian hymnody came out of a folk culture, and the spiritual gives every evidence of living on in our tradition. Following the televising of Martin Luther King Jr.'s funeral service, Edwin Newman mused over the air to the effect that he wondered what King would think about the "quaint and old-fashioned" sermon his father had preached. It was reported that Newman received a torrent of letters in response, among them a number from sophisticated white theologians, protesting that comment. The white church has come to realize that many black preachers are masters at taking the stories of the Bible and uniquely applying them to our modern situation. Martin Luther King Sr. has that gift and many are realizing that that is not considered "quaint" but is rather the epitome of what good modern preaching is all about. Consider also the impact that the Rev. Jesse Jackson is having on educators today by his telling young black people that the only way they are going to learn reading, writing, and arithmetic is by sweat and hard work. Learning, he says, is only fun when we have invested a good deal of perspiration in its accomplishment. The contribution of black Christians to the American church is enormous. When we fully learn to appreciate that contribution, we will be so much more enriched. This is one example of the benefits of culture caring.

We no doubt have made some strides in better appreciating the contributions of blacks to our society and church. This does not mean we do not have a good way to go. Color-coding and the results of racism stubbornly refuse eradication. One of our prominent black pastors visited an evangelism conference a few years ago. He came late and slipped into a back pew. During a break a white woman rushed up to him and gushed, "and you must be one of our African friends!"

"No, I was born in Ohio, madam," he replied softly. Startled, she dropped his hand and quickly went searching for a more compatible human being with whom to share Christian fellowship. One of the strange sides of our color-coding is our willingness to accept people of different hues if they originate from overseas, but not if they have been born on American soil. As the story of the Good Samaritan should tell us, culture caring ought to begin at home.

One of the most striking developments in worldwide Christian gatherings and organizations is to see how prominent the people from churches in Asia, Latin America and Africa have become. Whether it is in the more recent assemblies of the Lutheran World Federation, the World Council of Churches or the World Alliance of Evangelicals, leaders from the Third World are being heard. They make good sense. They keenly perceive where the church's mission ought to be going. Many unmask the Scriptures in new ways. Perhaps this is because their cultures are closer to the cultures from which the Bible emerged. It is no doubt a combination of many factors. It is clear that God is using these brothers and sisters to bless the churches of Europe and North America. This is another reason we should be in the business of culture caring.

There are other ways in which culture caring can enrich our church. I belong to a denomination that is still quite rural in its makeup. Its membership is concentrated in five states of the Upper Midwest. I am often startled by the lack of understanding existing between rural and urban folks. There are city people who actually believe country people are ignorant. Recently I visited a parishioner who is a large pork producer. I was freshly reminded of the intricacies of this operation and the sophistication with which it must be executed. It takes an enormous amount of knowledge about feed, biology, accounting, planting, fertilizers, and marketing in order to survive in almost any type of farming today. That same afternoon I had been asked to address a group of college professors. My opening gambit to them, still impressed with the hog farmer's skills, was: "If you fellows knew as much about your academic discipline as this pork producer knows about his work, you would all be teaching at Harvard."

That occasioned a discussion about my experience and they all admitted to a scanty knowledge about how intricate farming really is today. Since then, several of them have taken time to go out and visit a farm or two. Their respect is growing. Many images we hold of the farmer whether current or those of a bygone era are erroneous. As one agricultural economist contends, the farmer has always been, and still is, the most creative and efficient producer in the history of this nation. The agricultural sector has increased its productive capacities manyfold over other sectors in our economy. Someone describes the farmer as one who constantly has "the future in his eyes and the present in his hands." That would be my definition of intelligent Christian caring.

But it is also true that there is a great amount of misunderstanding in rural areas about urban life. Some of this results from inappropriate fear. The city does not seem to embrace any of the virtues of the God-given earth. Some feel God deserted the city and left it to its own devices. It is fascinating to watch the metamorphosis that takes place when we regularly bring a group of rural youth to get acquainted with their counterparts in the center city. They bring with them all the myths they have absorbed, but in a couple of hours, most of these dissipate and our young people begin to respond to the humanness of their newly-found urban acquaintances. Fears evaporate. These young men and women begin to get clues about the complexity of living in the city and gain appreciation for what the church seeks to do to minister there. One visit does not a believer make, but it begins to set in motion a whole new pattern of thought. They learn that God gives grace to people to adapt creatively to the demands of urban living; this seems to be especially true of the poor. We need more urban-rural dialogs leading to a greater appreciation of the church's unity in diversity.

Another area where we are learning about culture caring is the women's role in our society. In a sense, there is a men's and women's culture. It is dawning on many males how really sexist their attitudes have been. This is a particularly important lesson for the church. Our congregational constitutions, our liturgies, our leadership patterns, and our clergy are far too permeated with male-oriented reference points. Some things are being done, but more must be undertaken. A secular anthropologist contends that unless the church takes this situation seriously, it will not survive as an institution in Western society. Some people even seem to be amused by this whole movement and dismiss it as a fad. How deeply this liberation has affected us can be illustrated in the confusion many men now have about the male role. The women's movement gives every indication of deeply affecting the church in all its parts. Some of the agonizing reappraisal it is causing might be illustrated in a line from George Gobel: "I run my home like a ship; I'm the captain. How did I know I was going to marry an admiral?" We should thank God that many women are taking on the "admirable" trait of standing up to define their rights. That will eventually liberate the men of the church as well.

Appreciation for the many contributions of diverse elements and groups in the life of the church can only bind us closer together. The Scriptures promise that. Culture caring will only make the body more agile and fit for accomplishing Christ's mission in our day. Appreciation of cultural differences in the church is not a luxury to enjoy but a necessity to expect.

# 5

# Caring for
# the Ninety Percent

*You have come to fulness of life
in him who is the head of all rule
and authority* (Col. 2:10).

I have a friend who has contributed richly to
many phases of the church's life. Many times I heard
him remark: "God cares just as much about the
ninety percent, you know." He spoke from the perspective of a layperson who had heard numerous
clergymen speak about the need for proportionate
giving as if the only thing God really cared about
was the tithe.

Caretakers are concerned not only for the tithe
portion of their money they pledge to give. Caretakers know they receive all their gifts, money, prop-
erty, and possessions from God the gracious Giver.
They live in the confidence that God cares about
them and their time, income and daily needs. The
Psalmist says He "neither slumbers nor sleeps" (Ps.

121) and watches over us twenty-four hours of every day.

The earliest Christian creed was simply the confession: "Jesus is Lord!" By that is meant that Jesus is ruler of all the universe and he is *my* Lord. He is not Lord over some of my life, but over all. This idea is expressed beautifully in the first chapter of Colossians (verses 15-20). If one could hear that section read aloud in Greek, the staccato-like repetition of "ta panta" (all things) would build like the sound of the timpani giving crescendo to a symphony's triple forte climax. All things, says Colossians, exist to praise the Lord Christ. Though it may not appear that way to us much of the time, all things are subject to his domination. "All things" includes our checkbook.

What might happen if we became serious in our concern for the ninety percent in our parishes? (A new guidebook to help congregations and their members with responsible use of the ninety percent is *A Community of Stewards,* an ALC Momentum for Mission resource available from Augsburg Publishing House.) We could bring in financial experts to teach us how to prepare a budget and stick with it. We might have someone knowledgeable talk to us about the right kinds of investments to make. That might not be a bad idea, and financial institutions often provide such services. Yet there are some moral and value questions involved in the way we consume and spend. Not much help is being given in areas like my response to advertising, my understanding of quality products, and my penchant for buying the unnecessary. Here we could utilize someone, Christian or no, who has adopted a simplified living style. Many young people know a great deal about the phony advertisements and products that abound in so great a profusion today.

We do have a responsibility to be better informed about the deceptions and trickery of the advertising world. Otherwise why would a store manager's blush at being found squeezing toilet paper sell so much of that product? Why do beautiful girls draped over the hood of a car make us feel good about the engineering of that particular automobile? Why does a cat that can do the cha-cha-cha sell so much pet food? Why should ominous warnings about "ring around the collar" cause us to rush over to the nearest supermarket to buy a preventive detergent?

Perhaps we are becoming inured to silly ad gimmicks. A whole batch of products, however, is being sold under false pretenses. Claims that are dangerously misleading are aired with little protest. Is our unconcern about such things not an offense to God who entrusts money to us to spend wisely and well? We need people in our congregations who will do the research and compare notes to make us wiser consumers and better stewards. This might be a good project for a young couples' club, as studies indicate that most advertisers make their pitch to the under-thirty-five group since these people are more ready to try something different than older people.

Since stewardship patterns are formed in the very young, we might concentrate on the brainwashing being given to young children on Saturday morning

TV. The appeal is not sublimated and is obviously effective. The group known as Action for Children's Television (46 Austin St., Newtonville, Mass. 02160) has a fine track record. It has succeeded in reducing weekend commercial advertising during children's programs from sixteen minutes to nine and a half minutes per hour. ACT has ended advertising of all medicines and vitamins on children's TV and put a halt to the practice of having the hosts of children's programs do the actual advertising. It has done good work in reducing violence, along with racial and sexual stereotyping. It is now trying to deal with the enormous number of sweetened products sold on Saturday mornings. It has documented that in one seven hour period there were sixty-seven ads for sugared products. Several church groups have profited by using the materials ACT produces.

Even more to the point of our caretaking responsibility is the need for Christians to come together in groups to search out which products have quality and which do not. This would take a great deal of time, but could be of exceptional value to member families. We know about planned obsolescence in general, but what about the particular products we use? Many people are on a financial treadmill because of the need to replace major household items. Such research and sharing of findings could serve as a major part of the church's stewardship education program.

We pick on TV because it has such a major influence on people's lives. Not only the advertising should give us pause, and the violence and sex; but an even spookier effect ought to be examined. It has to do with the stewardship of time and abilities. Major studies are now showing the devastating influence the many hours children watch TV is having upon their learning. They are becoming ever more lethargic when they enter the classroom. Teachers even complain about such quality shows as *The Electric Company* and *Sesame Street* as having a debilitating effect on learning. Children expect to be entertained in their schools just as they are by the tube. Reading and math skills, as Jesse Jackson reminds us, take hard work, and children are massively resisting such tasks. There is a noticeable lack of creativity in what they do, and their appetites for learning seem jaded or almost nonexistent.

One of the families of our congregation has taken the drastic action of cutting off TV altogether. It met with howls of protest at first, but not any more. The kids are beginning to draw and construct things again. They are finding creative ways of playing together. Most important, the family is renewing friendship and doing many more activities together. That may be too drastic an action as there are also many valuable and educational programs to watch. We most often do not realize, however, the way TV has been rearranging our lives until we actually shut down the tube for a period of time.

Caretaking parents are limiting the amount of time their children are allowed to watch TV. Considering the effects of "overwatch," this is a discipline that will make children wiser stewards in later life.

What we are saying is that God is concerned about all areas of our everyday lives. Perhaps nothing is so revealing of the priorities in a caretaker's life as is the checkbook. *Sixty Minutes,* the TV magazine, and usually a *good* example of TV programming, had a segment devoted to the checkbook revelation. A man claimed that he could tell almost everything about a family's life by simply examining their checks for a three-month period. Without knowing anything else about the families he studied, he had an uncanny knowledge of the family's lifestyle and the individual members within it. Though most of us would not have the skill of this expert, it might be very instructive for someone in the family to study the way the money was spent over the last several weeks. The checkbook is a pretty good indicator of our caretaking abilities.

Now by saying that God is concerned about the other nine-tenths of our spending patterns, we must realize he is also concerned about the remaining one-tenth. Jesus is Lord of all of our life. What can we say about the "tithe"? We know that it is a word primarily associated with the Old Testament. Some feel it is too legalistic to speak of giving a tenth since we live with a new covenant. Christ does not wish that we be slavish adherents to a set of rules and ceremonies.

The idea of consecrating a tenth of one's income to God is found among many nations of antiquity besides the Jewish people. For the Jews the Mosaic Law required that the fruits of the ground and the cattle be subject to tithing. The tithe of grain and fruit were sold and a slightly higher than market value of that tenth portion was given to God, while in the case of animals every tenth one was selected and committed to God. It is not always clear as to whether there were several tithes or just one. At times the tithe was brought to the temple and at other times it was kept in storage in the various villages. It was used to support the Levites and other needy people. It is clear that there were many points in Jewish history where the tithe was not paid. One of the reforms of Hezekiah was to demand that this custom be reestablished and the response was so hearty that new chambers had to be found to place the tithes of the people (2 Chron. 31:4-12). Malachi rebuked the people "for robbing God" by withholding offerings (Mal. 3:7-11).

Jesus chided the religious leaders of his time for their ostentation in presenting their tithes. He nowhere makes giving a tenth of one's income a "demand." Christians are free to go far beyond that.

The New Testament stresses proportionate giving in returning directly to God a measure of the bounty he daily supplies us. Paul seems to be cautious in suggesting what proportion should go directly to the causes of the church and others in need. He suggests at one point that the church at Corinth should have a plan that involves regularity, is inclusive of all members, and is proportionate to its means: "Every Sunday each of you must put aside some money, in proportion to what he has earned . . ." (1 Cor. 16:2). In his second letter to the same congregation, he encourages further gifts but is careful to state that "God will accept your gift on the basis of what you have to give, not on what you don't have" (2 Cor. 8:12).

What percentage should I give to my church? Each of us must answer that question for ourselves, but there are certain things we must take into account. The clear call in the New Testament is that our giving should be on a proportionate basis. Every Christian should know what proportion he or she is giving. Whenever I have talked with people about this on a one-to-one basis, they are always surprised at what percentage they come up with. It is usually around two percent or less. Some, of course, are in the dollar a Sunday bracket, evidently believing that what was good enough for grandpa is good enough for me.

I usually suggest to people that if they are serious about percentage giving, they might begin with the five percent figure. That usually is not overwhelming even to a young couple just starting out. Then I suggest further that they make an effort to increase that by one percent every year or two. Most people find that that method gets them up to the tithe rather painlessly, and many go beyond.

There are two basic reasons why we should not be reluctant to speak about the ten percent of our income. First, it is clear that Christ has the right to expect sacrifice from his followers since his sacrifice on the cross was total. Can we not admit that there is precious little sacrificing going on among our members? Some sacrifice more for their service club or bowling team than they do for Christ's mission.

The other reason we cannot be apologetic in speaking about proportionate giving is that by doing so we deny many the *joy* of giving. I have never met an unhappy tither. I have spoken with hundreds of people about giving and just have not run into anyone who has regrets or is resentful about giving ten percent or more to the Lord. I have found that literally scores of people who give that one dollar a Sunday or who are in the one or two percent category seem to resent every nickel they give. They have either been shamed into giving something or want to keep up some kind of appearance. God does not need or want that kind of giving. The tither is a "cheerful (the original Greek word is *hilarious)* giver" (2 Cor. 9:7).

Jesus is Lord over all areas of our life. He wants caretakers who are responsible for what they spend in their everyday living—the ninety percent; and he wants us to enjoy what we give to the program of his kingdom.

My church body a couple years ago put on a drive for mission endeavors both at home and abroad. The goal was $25 million; pledges exceeded $37 million. When the congregation I presently serve received its "suggested" goal for that appeal, it decided the latter was too low. So this group raised over three times the suggested objective. That happened in hundreds of congregations with even more spectacular results.

Could it be that there is a new momentum for mission developing among caretakers in America? Could it be that there is a new appreciation for mission beyond ourselves? Is it possible that we are taking better care of our day-to-day family expenses so that we can extend ourselves through gifts to others with greater need?

God wants one hundred percent caretakers.

# 6

# Care Taking
# and Care Giving

> *For if a man does not know how
> to manage his own household,
> how can he care for church?*
> (1 Tim. 3:5).

When we say, upon leaving friends, "Take care
. . .", we are saying two things as was suggested
in the pre-word. One, we are telling our friends that
we want them to take care of themselves and their
life because we love them and want them to remain
healthy and stay around for a long time. We are also
saying to them that we desire that they take care of
everything they touch in this world. We want them
to be caring of the earth and the people they affect.
We suggested that the former meaning has to do
with care *taking*, while the latter suggests care *giving*. Both are important to the Christian. In a somewhat imprecise sense, care taking has to do with the
ninety percent of our checkbook, while that part of

our income and energies that reaches out to others
has to do with care giving. Christian caretakers both
*take* care and *give* care.

We might illustrate these two kinds of caring by
looking at two distinct ways of thinking. In the last
decade a considerable amount of research has been
done on the processes of creative thought. Profiles
have been drawn up on the creative person. Tests
are being constructed to measure the creative potential of different individuals. The traditional Intelli-
gence Quotient (I.Q.) test does not measure creativity very well. Students of the way people think
call the more traditional measuring test, the I.Q.,
the measure of a person's ability to think conver-
gently, or more conventionally. Creativity is often
called divergent thinking. It really has little to do
with novelty, or thinking of something that has a
new approach or wrinkle to the thought; creativity
is just different from more conventional thought.
Researchers in creativity are saying that it has most
to do with those people who want desperately to get
something out of their head and heart and to have
that idea accomplished and put into some tangible
form. It may be a work of art, like a piece of sculp-
ture that is born in a person's head but must be
formed by hands shaping a piece of clay or marble.
It may be some writing like a short story that the
writer will move heaven and high water to express
in a form acceptable to himself. It could be a football play that is nothing until it is conveyed to
eleven players and executed on the gridiron. Creativity has to do with completing a task perhaps at

great cost to the creator. The creative person will not rest until his dream has been actualized and put into tangible form.

Profiles of a creative person picture him as one who works in spurts of uninterruptable fervor, is usually more concerned about the present than the future, and has a hopelessly littered desk. He seems to be possessed by an almost irrational passion for the task at hand and is determined, resolute, and persistent. One of the first home calls I made as a pastor was with a family who had a little girl whom they were trying to break of the habit of asking for a glass of water at bedtime. After the mother had come down from bedding the child, it was perhaps inevitable that the voice should come piping down the stairs, "Mommy, I want a glass of water." My hosts told me to ignore that cry, and we self-consciously tried to go on with our visit. After about three more attempts by that requesting little voice, the mother went to the head of the stairs and said loudly: "If I hear one more peep out of you, Janice, I am coming up to give you a spanking!" There was silence both upstairs and downstairs for a few moments when again the quiet was broken with the plea, "Mommy, when you come upstairs to give me a spanking, will you *please* bring me a glass of water?" Now, by the above standards, that was one creative little girl!

In describing two different ways of thinking, I am not placing a pejorative judgment on one or the other. We need people who can think more conventionally and traditionally, who are convergent thinkers. But we also need the divergent and creative thinkers. The tragedy is that our schools, by the use of I.Q. tests to the exclusion of any other, fail to affirm those who think primarily in the creative mode. Studies also show that many businesses allow room only for the more traditional thinker, while creative people are often considered round pegs in square holes. The person who does not fit into the organizational boxes may be the very person who could cause that organization to make a great leap forward.

A few years ago I conducted a series of research studies, comparing highly intelligent adolescents from the suburbs with young people in inner city schools who had made some special mark in their school, even if it was not primarily in academic pursuits. The differences were quite startling. The suburban youth were very verbal and articulated complicated theories in an impressive fashion. We asked the center city young people some questions in the same areas and found them to be much more concerned with solving problems. They clearly demonstrated greater adeptness at coping with situations the suburban youth did not even want to discuss. The youth who were out of a survival culture and lived to a great extent on the street were pragmatic "copers." They knew what it took to survive. Those living in a more regulated life-style were good at remembering what was in their textbooks and savored conversation that dealt primarily with ideas. This very ability to cope has prompted one industrial researcher to comment: "We hire kids from the inner city to carry boxes and sweep the floors, when they probably ought to be put in the center of a management team where their ability to wrestle with intractable problems could be invaluable."

Taking care of my life and all that surrounds it calls for my applying a certain amount of conventional wisdom. It means doing many of the same things the same way I did them yesterday. My daily work, health, nurture, and general tending to my world of existence basically demands a normal, steady, and conventional stewardship. That kind of care is necessary and useful. Sometimes it seems to be merely a plodding stewardship of that which God has bestowed upon me. Performing those tasks that are routine rather than exciting is a part of my discipleship. We should not put down that kind of caring. We see too little of it.

Now *giving* care might be compared to the more creative thinking. Giving care means reaching out to others beyond my world to extend a helping hand. That is tricky business. Caring, in the wrong way, could smother the other person. The mission of Christ today seems to demand the creative approach. Here the old ways are not necessarily the best ways. The attitude that says, "But we have always done it that way before," may only impede the church's mission. It is of the nature of things that when we seek to reach into another culture with a helping hand, we cannot form that hand in the same way as we might when working with people in our particular society. Some of the more exciting mission endeavors going on in the world today are ingenious in their ability to take small inputs and to allow them to spin off with reverberating effects.

We have said that evangelism and social concern are both ways of giving care. Rather than using formulas and timeworn procedures, these elements of our personal outreach, as well as that of the church, ought to be injected with as much creativity as God endows us. So much is at stake when we attempt to give our care to others.

One of the standard and conventional ways of witnessing to Jesus Christ in this country has been the evangelistic crusade or meeting. The Institute for American Church Growth of Pasadena, California, in studying several campaigns in recent months found that only three percent of those who "made decisions" became church members. The Institute director, Win Arn, says the only reliable measure of the effectiveness of mass evangelism is the number of people who become "responsible church members." The reliability of that study is attested to by many students of church life. Now we can rejoice about the three percent, but it is sobering to think how much harder it will be to reach the ninety-seven percent who evidently did not carry through with their intent. It is a rather frightening statistic. Would this not indicate that we must apply greater creativity to the ways in which we reach out to give care? Maybe the old campaign techniques with their well-ordered hymn sing warm-ups, elaborately decorated stages, expensively attired preachers, and messages calculated to lead to the right moment of decision-making lack the creative energy to reach people deeply for Christ.

Creative care giving calls for commitment, the kind of commitment that we spoke of earlier that just has to get the job done. Creative commitment gets that short story in print, sculpts until that form is completed, executes the play until it works against all opposition. There are many evidences of new stirrings among many who are dedicating themselves to their Lord. I have found that many newly-found charismatics are the most reliable people available when a tough task of social action must be effected. They seem to know that the Spirit of God is always ready to work his work of grace.

Care givers are the graceful creators of love. They know that it is only by grace that Jesus performs his acts of mercy on behalf of others. But in our staunch reliance upon grace, have we forgotten Jude's warning about exchanging the grace of God for liscentiousness (Jude 4)? Or what about Paul's question: Shall we sin that grace may abound? (Rom. 6:1). There is nothing creative about sin. It follows the old paths and trods the beaten highways. The self-deceit of sin only boxes us into the same old ground that closes doors to self-actualization and creative bursts of freedom and service.

We should be grateful to God for every creative representative of ours overseas who is giving care in such a way as to be a "cutting edge" for the church. There is, for instance, Bill Peters, who is working under the church's auspices engaged in community development in the Cameroon. Most of his efforts are in the small villages where agriculture is a central concern. He assists in the development of new varieties of food crops, the raising of chickens, training oxen for plowing, and in marketing and transporting these products. In India, through Lutheran World Relief, we are involved in a number of integrated rural development programs. In Balarampur and Sundarban, LWF representatives improve farming with health and sanitation programs, and create family industries and marketing plans. The list of small, creative programs for giving care to the physical and spiritual needs of others is a long one. These programs are being emulated by others so that their efforts are multiplied manyfold.

Taking care and giving care are two sides of one coin. When we approach both tasks in an appropriate way, we spend the coin of Christ's realm wisely and well.

# 7

# Giving Care a Perspective

> *Then the righteous will answer him, "Lord, when did we see thee hungry and feed thee, or thirsty and give thee drink . . . or a stranger . . . or naked . . . sick . . . or in prison?"* (Matt. 25:37-39).

The great fact of our time is the monumental disparity of resources between the southern and northern hemispheres.

Some years ago someone introduced me to an audience as the "hunger nut of the Lutheran church." The title follows me to this day. I do not mind being tabbed in this way as I am convinced that world hunger is the single most challenging issue ever to face the Christian church. A person can only hold one concern deep in his innards during a lifetime and this concern took hold of me many years ago. It happened on a trip around the world, mostly

to countries in the southern hemisphere. The specter of thousands of malnourished bodies dying by
inches is a scene never to be erased from a person's
memory.

The reason this is not a one-track issue is that it
incorporates so many other concerns under its vast
dome. Other issues—like race, the role of women, the
Church's mission, ecology, methods of evangelism,
economic justice, rich and poor tensions, ecumeni-
city, treatment of minorities, the interpretation of
Scripture—all pertain in some way to the understanding of the complex tangle of concerns represented
by the hunger question.

Is it, as has been suggested, "the single most challenging issue ever to face the Christian church"?
The church faced and survived a great many crises.
The early church had to combat the sprawling do-
main of Rome as well as insistent heresies in its own
midst. It had to survive the Constantine threat of the
fourth century. It lived through the Dark Ages and
even came through the schismatic Reformation and
the rationalism of the Enlightenment. It faced the
missionary challenge of the nineteenth century by
covering the globe with the Gospel message. It
managed in this century to turn criticism of the
scriptural documents into a deeper understanding of
the biblical message. The more recent "God is dead"
theologians barely caused a ripple. I would contend
that these challenges can hardly be compared with
the magnitude of meeting the needs of a billion
people who suffer from lack of essentials for human
dignity, from malnutrition, and from starvation.

Some of the previous challenges to the church to care, admittedly, were different in nature. In some ways the magnitude of the challenge rich Christians must assume in carrying the burdens of the poor in our day is most similar to the enormous task the early church had in evangelizing the then-known world.

Perhaps the title of this chapter could be slightly changed to "Giving Care: A Perspective." The challenge of our time is to find that focus that is beyond ourselves. Without apology I would say that for us it must be to hold fast to a perspective that will enable us to reach out to our hungry brothers and sisters. This is a complicated topic. Yet gaining some kind of perspective on it releases us to act in ways which could be significant for both the rich and the poor.

To gain that perspective one of the first steps is to root out the underbrush that obscures the hunger question. For there are many myths that confuse our vision of the hungry. Here are some of the most prominent:

"If they would start to control their population growth, maybe we could begin to help them," says one myth. Lack of birth control is not the primary culprit creating the tremendous growth in population since World War II. We did not reach the first billion in world population until 1830. The next billion came in another hundred years. By 1960, only thirty years later, we added the third billion; and we surpassed the fourth billion by the mid-seventies.

Why the tremendous rate of growth in these later years? Primarily it was due to "death control" because of D.D.T., the hygienic procedures, and miracle drugs, most all of which came out of the Second World War. Babies that once most certainly would die, now live. Many nations have introduced massive programs to quell their growth. China has turned the tide of newborn babies around. Many Moslem nations such as Indonesia, Pakistan and Egypt that had a more deeply-held taboo on birth control than many Christians, have introduced effective programs of control. India has begun controversial programs of sterilization in some of its states. Most cities in India display large posters encouraging birth control, and the country has increased its clinics for this purpose by manyfold. It is not as if these countries have not taken strong steps toward diminishing the number of births. The Population Institute indicated in 1978 that for the first time in history the rate of growth in the poor countries has turned downward. It is also true that demographers indicate that the only sure way to slow population growth is for a nation to raise its standard of living. That is what happened in Western nations. We in the United States are standing on the verge of zero population growth (ZPG) because, to put it bluntly, the more things families acquire, the less their desire for more children. For families in the Third World it is a matter of seeing that not so many of their babies die; and they want the children they have to receive a better chance. The famous KAP (Knowledge, Attitude, Population) studies prove that people in every area of the earth desire to keep their families small. This is especially true in Latin America where the myth of "macho man" is sharply receding.

The point is that we can no longer say these poorer nations are not trying to control population. Furthermore, if we could increase the amount of self-help assistance, that exponential growth would substantially slow down.

Another myth regarding hunger reads, "These people are lazy and backward, and do not want to help themselves." George Borgstrom of Michigan State has worked long and hard in the study of the world's poor and his tests show that malnutrition is the chief reason for most of these people's sluggishness at work. It is also impossible for someone to write a Horatio Alger story in places where virtually no opportunities exist. In many cases that opportunity has been taken away by colonial policies that left newly-independent nations bereft of an economic base.

It is not fair to assume that poor people do not want to help themselves. The favorite slogan from the Third World is: "We want justice, not charity." The newest United Nations organization, the UN Conference on Trade and Development (UNCTAD), largely formed by economically poor nations, has come up with many carefully developed programs to increase trading prospects between rich and poor nations. Though economists generally agree that these are sound proposals benefiting all who would participate, the proposals have been largely turned down by nations of the West and those under Soviet influence.

People in the southern hemisphere are fiercely proud. When they have a choice in the matter, they only want programs introduced into their country that give them the possibility of helping themselves.

"Most aid is wasteful and does not go to the people in real need," sums up a third myth. Now it seems everyone knows a horror story or two that tells of unconscionable waste or deliberate graft. The media have been very alert to these instances. What we forget oftentimes is that this wasting of aid is becoming increasingly impossible and represents only a tiny percentage of what goes overseas. Our Agency for International Development (AID) programs have been in operation for over a quarter of a century, and we have learned a great deal about circumventing the cheaters and eliminating the wasteful programs. I have worked with several AID personnel in recent years and am thoroughly impressed with their seasoned cleverness and deep desire to see that our programs work.

This care in seeing to it that aid reaches the neediest has always been basically true of our church-sponsored programs. After all, we most often operate in places where we already have representatives that know the people's need and know how to effect equitable distribution. There are some fly-by-night operators who go under a Christian name that deserve only prosecution, but they are exceptions.

A fourth myth declares, "We are already doing too much." Usually that refers to our foreign aid programs. Do most of us know how much we actually give in humanitarian aid to all nations? The last reliable figures are from 1975. In that year we spent $3.67 billion, and of that more than half went to military assistance with only $1.5 billion for economic development. Another $1.3 billion was spent for food, but the large portion of that, three-fourths in fact, was in the form of long-term loans, not gifts. That total has slightly increased recently but has not kept pace with our hefty military spending which is nearly fifty times as great. On the basis of the percentage of Gross National Product (GNP), we ranked fourteenth to sixteenth among the seventeen wealthiest nations in our aid giving for the past several years. Church World Service and Lutheran World Relief do yeoman service in meeting needs, but their efforts can only be a small fraction of what governments are able to do.

Well, if we are of a mind to act as Christians in the rich nation, what can we do?

First, I would say, we can be informed. There is a great deal of mythology running around about the hunger question. It is also true that one finds European laity considerably more knowledgeable about these issues than their American counterparts. Mostly that is due to the fine educational work by the churches of Europe. The average person on the street can speak most intelligently about this issue. The results bear this out as many nations in Europe do so much more per capita in public and private aid.

Every denomination now has a study course or two for groups who wish to be informed. A great deal of literature and audiovisuals are also available. One of the best volumes which takes the biblical message seriously is *Rich Christians in an Age of Hunger* by Ronald J. Sider. In addressing the rich Christians and their penchant for creating myths of rationalization, he says:

> In the coming decades rationalizations for our affluence will be legion. They will be popular and persuasive. . . . But all things are possible with God—if we will hear and obey his Word. If there is any ray of hope for the future, it is in the possibility that growing numbers of affluent Christians will dare to allow the Bible to shape their relationship to a billion sons and daughters of poor Lazarus" (p. 56).

This is a book crammed with current, factual data and with a perspective that correctly combines evangelical concern with sociopolitical witness.

Secondly, we can give. Though the media only turn the spotlight on this problem during an occasional famine abroad, we may be sure that the poor we shall "always have with us." The need is staggering, and while this may be discouraging, we cannot be given over to cynical futility. Our church agencies are ideal channels for our gifts of money. Their overhead is very low, in the neighborhood of eight to ten percent. This is because through congregations they have a ready-made network for informing people of needs, and do not have to buy expensive advertising in magazines or television. They cannot personalize our gifts as the orphaned children agencies do, but neither do they set up the involved administrative structure such operations demand. We can be sure, as we emphasized earlier, that our monetary gift goes to people in need. The church has networks overseas and can thereby insure delivery.

Our pocketbooks should open more often than just around Thanksgiving time. Some families place an old envelope gaily colored by the children on their living room table and bring a new envelope in monthly that is filled with contributions by all members of the family. It is a symbolic reminder of God's providential care for us. Another crucial way for people in the rich lands to respond to this need is to take part in political action. This rubs some people the wrong way. They say we should keep the church and state apart. Christianity and politics do not mix well. Or they would argue that individual Christians are called to exercise the precious privilege of voting and contacting their congressman. All of these statements have an element of truth to them. We do not want the sharp division of political power in relation to the church to erode. And we cannot glibly say that our political philosophy can always be blessed by our understanding of the faith. It is a part of our vocation to act as individuals to influence legislation. Not all issues on the political spectrum are as clear as our concern for the hungry. It is morally and theologically defensible that every Christian who professes love for the Lord Jesus will want to help the unfortunate of the earth.

Bread for the World involves both Protestant and Roman Catholic Christians in actions that are carefully thought out and effectively organized. A Christian can receive valuable information pertaining to poverty issues both here and abroad by sending for their monthly newsletter. Its Executive Director, Arthur Simon, is a Lutheran pastor long devoted to this cause. One does not live in Washington, D.C., very long before one realizes that there is a lobby group for every single cause on God's green earth. Except for groups like Bread for the World, those living on parched earth around the world have no voice raised on their behalf.

Another way in which caretakers can express their concern is to take action in an area nearer home. Perhaps this is an Indian reservation or a metropolitan area not too distant from your parish. Domestic and world poverty are of a piece. Their causes are often similar, and suffering always takes on the same grotesque shape.

Now this task of helping in our own country is the most difficult of all. For one thing, many poor people do not want another group meddling in their affairs. They have had quite a bit of that. It will mean that a group in the congregation will have to "pay their dues" over a period of time so that they are informed of the situation as well as can be and have taken time to develop a trust relationship. That comes hard. Often overtures will be rebuffed because of mistrust developed by other "do-gooders" who botched their chances. Also it will lead to a long-term commitment, as the poor are tired of fitful starts that lead nowhere. Yet this kind of action, when done well, can be the most fulfilling.

Finally, what do our members know about the world mission enterprise of our denomination? This comes under the category of being better informed, but it should mean more than that. We ought to be able to identify in what areas of the world our church is ministering to the whole person and in what way. There are even opportunities for certain members with special skills to give of themselves overseas as dentists, carpenters, teachers, doctors and as various agricultural advisors. Are there certain tasks overseas that our denomination is looking for young people to fill? What preparation will they need? Some nations are closing their doors to missionaries unless they bring with them special skills. These are the kinds of questions most world mission offices are glad to answer. So much is happening in our mission programs that we need to keep up with what is new and try to find ways in which on a long-term or short-term basis we can contribute. Many persons have time to give. Retired people are often at the prime of their life and could give of themselves in a most rewarding way. President Carter's mother and a whole host of dedicated persons have contributed their wisdom in this way.

The concern for the world's hungry can give proper perspective to all of our giving. It should cause us by its very dimension to think, study, pray, worship and act in ways that give substance to our caretaking.

# 8

# Moved to Care

> *With eyes wide open to the mercies of God, I beg you, my brothers [and sisters], as an act of intelligent worship, to give him your bodies, as a living sacrifice* . . . Romans 12:1-2a (Phillips).

What moves me to care? Why should I care at all?

There is an enduring illustration that is told in many different versions, the latest of which is contained in the popular song, "Tie a Yellow Ribbon on the Old Oak Tree." The original version I heard has to do with a rebellious son who cannot abide his parents control and runs off to join the navy. He receives a great deal of sea duty and visits many of the ports of the world expressing his freedom and seeking his fun. Meanwhile the parents try to track him down and regularly send letters to him, but

these all return unopened. One day, sitting aboard
ship in mid-Atlantic, the boy realizes how much he
yearns to be reconciled with his parents, and sits
down and writes a long letter. Now we find him on
a train nervously awaiting the next stop which is
his hometown. He is sitting next to a pastor who
sees how the young man fidgets and appears distraught.

"What is the trouble, son?" the pastor asks. Visibly
relieved by a contact from someone who seems to
care, the boy tells the whole story. "And you see,
Pastor, I told my parents that I did not expect them
to welcome me back home, but if they wanted me to
stop and see them, I asked that they place a white
rag on one of the front branches of the apple tree in
our yard and I would see it from the train window
and get off. But I'm afraid to look." The pastor sees
that the train is slowing and almost feverishly looks
for the cottage the boy had described and for that apple tree. After a few moments, the pastor's face breaks
into a wide smile and he turns to the young man
and says, "I don't think you have to worry, son, you
see there is a white rag tied to every single branch
of that apple tree." That is what Paul means by
having our "eyes wide open to the mercies of God."
In effect, God ties a white rag to every branch of the
apple tree when he reveals to us the merciful forgiveness of the cross.

The cross and the cross alone, moves us to care.

A few years ago Frank Reynolds of the American
Broadcasting Company hosted an interview series
with some of the leading religious lights of our time.

One memorable program consisted of Reynolds asking Rabbi Abraham Heschel what he understood
sin to be. Heschel was slow to respond, but in his
own thoughtful manner he said in effect: "You
know, some of my closest friends are Christian theologians (sound familiar?—only in his case, he truly
meant it), but they have done a great disservice to
the understanding of the fall of Adam and Eve. They
have most often said that the basic sin as revealed
in the story was pride. Oh, some theologians inter-
pret the basic sin to be the sexual drive, but most
often it has been described as some type of ego-
building. From the earliest times, rabbis have been
saying that the story of the snake and the apple and
the first parents reveals that the most basic sin was
deceit, and more especially, *self*-deceit." He went
on to point out that every detail of that story had
to do with a process of self-imposed deception.

That insight set off a revolution within me. It is
true that if I somehow peel off the layers of sin in
my life, I finally come to one ugly fact: that I am
constantly fooling others and in that process, deceiv-
ing myself. God must continually strip away our
masks to let us see ourselves as we are.

That understanding of the basic sin and of the
purpose of the Law has been most helpful to me. I
find I need to hear what God expects of me again
and again. I can find more ways to fool myself than
I dreamed were possible, not to mention how I seek
to deceive others. Along with that understanding I
realize that hearing only God's expectations in the
Law can leave me paralyzed and in despair.

When the Bible uses the term, "the Law," as, for example, in Romans 1–8, it embraces more than the Ten Commandments. Though students of jurisprudence make the point that every civil law ever enacted can be traced back to the Decalogue, "the Law" is any word that calls us to achieve or do better. Advertisements are most-often Law. They sometimes try to shame us to buy a product. An example of this method is an ad playing on the embarrassment a housewife is supposed to feel because her present floor wax leaves an inexcusable "ugly yellow build-up" on her floor. An entire satire on soap operas was created around that ad. When you listen closely to most of these ads, even those that seem somewhat playful, they have a bite that is not hidden too deeply. They say, like the Law always says, "Why can't you do better?"

Most graduation speeches proclaim lofty ideals that would seem to be unattainable by ninety-nine percent of the class. In fact, most of the signals that schools send out to their students are law-oriented. It is a deep-seated belief in our society that that is the only way to get young people to "shape up."

The Law, in and of itself, does not move us to do anything. We should be quite clear about this. The Law convicts, needles, wounds, destroys, puts down, consumes, ruins, slays and distresses. It places us in prison. It shows us what we are. The Law strips away our defenses by ripping off the masks of pretense and delusion. Finally, it goes to the heart of our trouble by revealing to us our self-deception.

Almost everywhere we go we are pummeled by what we ought to be doing, and doing better.

Thus, more than ever, we need to hear repeatedly the uplifting music of the Gospel, the Good News. In the very machinations of our self-deception, we hear the rescuing word of forgiveness from Christ. "I accept you even when you try to hide yourself from yourself," he says. "I do not ask of you that you promise never to wear another mask: I ask only that you let me reach down and embrace you in the midst of your delusion." It is the Gospel of God's love and forgiveness that moves us and changes us. The Gospel builds, heals, encourages, restores, replaces, repairs, renews, revives and gives us new life. That is what moved the parents and the boy in the story at the beginning of this chapter. Only when our eyes are wide open to the mercies of God, are we impelled into caring for others.

An old sage has said that "the boatman reaches the landing partly by pulling, partly by letting go; the archer strikes his target partly by pulling, partly by letting go." We may push ourselves forward all we can by means of striving to keep the Law, but when we learn to let go of our masks and the facade of self-deception, God can show us his grace. That is when the love of God sweeps in to forgive. That is when we understand how deeply Jesus cared through his cross. A favorite expression of a beloved, now deceased, seminary professor, George Aus, was: "Let go and let God!"

It is the Gospel that moves us to care.

More often than not, we are tempted to motivate

giving by means of the Law rather than the Gospel. William Hordern makes the point in his book, *Living by Grace,* that Protestants are more likely to rely on "works righteousness" in the practice of church life than upon the motivating power of the Gospel.

> A church that believed in justification and was freed from its fear for the preservation of the institution would develop its stewardship so that it enhanced the credibility of the doctrine of justification. Such a church would believe not only that God loves a cheerful giver (2 Cor. 9:7) but also that God desires no other kind of giver. Therefore, it would make no effort to beg, cajole, or entice the recalcitrant to give to the church. . . . Those who were filled with the love of God would cheerfully give for those activities that seemed to serve God. If such an approach did not bring sufficient funds to keep the institution of the church going, then it could well be concluded that the institution was so near failing in its purpose for existence that it could without loss be allowed to die. That seems exactly what Luther had in mind when he said that it would be better to let the church die than to resort to fear to get people to support it (pp. 183-184).

We need to be more honest in the church about our giving care. That much the Law can do. It is painfully honest. But we are also desperately in need of that which can motivate us to mission: the Gospel. As we reflect on the stewardship appeals made in our congregations, upon what have most of those appeals rested? The Law seems the most effective. There comes the Old Deceiver once again deluding us to believe that the Law can truly motivate people by telling them what they should do. But demands of the Law cannot, and do not, move us to care. Only the Gospel releases us to be the people of God moving forward with a sense of purpose.

If it is the Gospel that moves us, why are not more people moving? For years parish reports coming into denominational headquarters reveal that most churches divide their giving by spending eighty percent on themselves and giving twenty percent away. The *Church Financial Statistics and Related Data 1977* indicates that forty-four U.S. communions averaged 20.8% in giving to benevolences. Most people would agree that that is not a very good balance. Certainly one ideal would be a fifty-fifty congregation, giving at least half of their funds to people less fortunate outside the boundaries of their parish. One basic reason why we as churches do not stretch out with missionary hands is that we have a hard time hearing the "Go" in the Gospel. The Law registers quickly and deeply. The Gospel we resist because we just have to find some way to justify ourselves.

In the late fifties the youth departments of several Lutheran bodies joined in an ambitious study of the problems, attitudes, and dreams of both young and old which led to the publishing of *A Study of Generations* (Augsburg, 1972). Several years went into its preparation, and the result was as accurate an instrument for measuring problems and attitudes as had up to that time been developed. One of the findings caused particular concern among parents, teachers, and pastors. It was, in effect, that our Lu-

theran young people were living under the Law.
Under the apparent carefree, bouncy exterior there
lurked a great deal of fear and guilt. Few found joy,
contentment and assurance in the promises of Christ.
A majority of the youth tested expressed a fear of
God, and of death, and an uncertainty about their
faith. Indications are that that has not appreciably
changed in almost a generation since the first testing
was done. For a church that has emphasized the
Gospel that frees from sin and unites people to
Christ, that is alarming. It corroborates the impression many of us have who have been at camps, con-
ventions and leadership schools and who can get
quite close to young people, since they know we
do not follow them back to their home communities.

Why do people have such a hard time hearing the
Gospel? For starters, we should remind ourselves
that there is, as Paul said so often (e.g., Gal. 5:11), a
scandal to the cross. It runs counter to everything
conventional religious wisdom teaches. The Law ac-
commodates to our desire to moralize about Jesus
and it fits comfortably with our desire to contribute
some small thing to our salvation. In addition the
Law is heard everywhere. Whether it be the magazine or TV ads or much of the literature we read, or
convocation speakers urging to greater heights of
achievement, the strains of the Law create a cacoph-
ony of sound that says: "You must be better than
you are and do better than you are doing!" Perhaps
we do not hear the Gospel because we try to hedge
it around with conditions. As a pastor, I know how
easy it is to avoid the radicality of proclaiming this

Good News. It seems so much more sensible to put some clothes around that naked Gospel so it will appear more presentable.

However, when that still, small voice strikes deeply into our heart that we are freed and forgiven, it releases us to be new persons. One of the ways our freedom becomes most apparent is in a new desire to care for others. If he cares that much about me, he surely cares about others. All the old cliches like "taking care of number one" lose their appeal. It is the Gospel that releases us to be on a mission. How we need to hear that word again and again!

One summer before I entered the seminary I was invited to be a student pastor in two smaller congregations in North Dakota. I was to fill in until a new pastor should arrive. At the end of a very enriching experience one lady, who had said hardly anything to me during my stay, came up at the farewell party to tell me: "When I heard we were getting a student I was disappointed as we have had some good preachers here, but I vowed I would intently listen for any Gospel word I could receive. Even though you're young and not such a good preacher, I came away with a word of forgiveness every Sunday and I thank you." That compliment, such as it was, reminded me that there are always people listening for that good word from the cross. "For those who know it best seem hungering and thirsting to hear it like the rest." We cannot speak the Gospel too much in this Law-oriented world.

Whether the congregation is involved in a stewardship campaign, an evangelism program or a social concerns outreach, it is the rhythm of Law and Gospel, with a heavy emphasis on the latter that must accompany our work. There are people who need to hear the Law confronting them with their selfishness and greed. But far more often, people hunger and thirst for that radical Gospel, releasing them to be what God intends them to be.

As I write these words, the congregation I serve is in the midst of a stewardship emphasis. Previous to this, I have not seen such enthusiasm and diligence shown by a stewardship board, by the callers and by the congregation. The initial reports indicate we will substantially increase our budget that groans somewhat from the support of a full Christian Day School program. I am convinced it is the Gospel that has stirred the excitement and hard work. For the first time, we have a chance to turn our eyes outward and seriously consider the mission which is ours. I know I have not prior to this trusted enough in the promises of our Lord in the matter of a congregational budget. Again, God proved me wrong. A congregation that wishes to demonstrate that it cares immerses itself in the risks of the Gospel. Anything worth undertaking is achieved "with eyes wide open to the mercies of God."

Luther's favorite expression for the word "faith" was "confidence in the Divine Promises." In the matter of giving of ourselves or our resources, the promises of God are extravagant. He tells us that we shall "receive a full measure, a generous helping, poured into your hands—all that you can hold" (Luke 6:38 TEV).

# 9

## Quality Caring

*One thing is needful. Mary has
chosen the good portion. . . .*
(Luke 10:42).

We Americans are known for "thinking big." It
has enabled our nation to accomplish some impressive feats in industry, government, religion, the military and in a whole host of human endeavors for
social betterment. This kind of quantitative thinking
has led also to enormous waste. It leads us to pull
out the stops in production and distribution; and if
that leads to a scarcity of precious materials or the
erosion of non-renewable resources, we tend to justify this on the grounds that a big job is getting done.
Thinking of our waste of energy alone, some com-
mentators state, "the world cannot afford the United
States."

We are now much more conscious of our limita-
tions and seem to be returning to old-fashioned vir-

tues of thrift and simplicity. Some say, "thriftiness is next to godliness," or conservation is next to consecration. Is it not remarkable that so many people interested in conserving wish to get back to basic qualities of life, such as appreciation of the land, wildlife, and protecting natural habitats? There seems to be a yearning among city dwellers to return to a more pastoral life. More highly sought than ever are acreages and summer cabins in areas where population density is low and the natural order is great. One publisher that transcribes books to cassette tapes for listening by city commuters as they travel to and from work says that the tape most requested by these urbanites is Thoreau's *Walden.*

My father was not a man of great means, and he did not buy anything very often. But when he did purchase something for the children or our home, it was always of the very highest quality. "It always pays to buy the very best," I can remember him telling me repeatedly. His advice has stayed with me and I am still leery of buying merchandise which perhaps costs less, but has no lasting value. We still use household items in our present home that he purchased many years ago for my boyhood home.

A person can think quantitatively or qualitatively. To do the former means to be impressed with numbers, size and abundance. Qualitative thinking prizes that which has an intrinsic value of its own. We who live in the more affluent areas of the world unconsciously seem to think in quantitative terms. Current anthropological studies point out that same thing. The values of people living in the northern and richer areas of the globe emphasize quantity, while those of people in the older cultures of the south, who also happen to be poor, stress quality.

A few years ago I shared a motel room with an African Christian while attending a church conference. Some weeks before, it was reported that some color television sets emitted radiation that might be dangerous to viewers. In the back pages of the local newspaper one evening during that conference the paper reported that it would be too costly to take these sets out of production and therefore the government agency regulating this product found it unfeasible to take the sets off the market. My friend, reading this, commented, "But this is astounding! Do you mean to tell me that you value your technology above the safety of human beings?" It struck me that I had not been as troubled by the article as he. It also struck me that I was so immersed in the quantity of production that I was not as disturbed as I should have been when the quality of human beings were ignored.

It was with great interest that I discovered the writings of E. F. Schumacher. How much we have allowed quantitative thinking to control us, Schumacher illustrates in many ways.

> In the marketplace, for practical reasons, innumerable qualitative distinctions which are of vital importance for man and society are suppressed; they are not allowed to surface. Thus the reign of quantity celebrates its greatest triumphs in "The Market." Everything is equated with everything else. To equate things means to give them a price and thus to make them exchangeable. To the extent

that economic thinking is based on the market, it takes the sacredness out of life, because there can be nothing sacred in something that has a price. Not surprisingly, therefore, if economic thinking pervades the whole society, even simple non-economic values like beauty, health, or cleanliness can survive only if they prove to be "economic" (*Small Is Beautiful,* p. 43).

Contrary to what some think, Schumacher does not argue that everything in the social order must be scaled down. He does argue against the mentality that breeds a "mindless adulation of growth" and persuasively contends for scaling certain functions down so that we do not eliminate human necessities. Recently, economist Robert Heilbroner, who wrote the rather pessimistic, *Enquiry into the Human Prospect,* spoke in our city and, when asked what he thought about Schumacher, replied that he thought some of his ideas intriguing, but that he had too optimistic a view of human nature. He is right, of course. Christians need to be skeptical about anything that does not take sin seriously.

One's emphasis upon the qualitative takes the perversity of human nature seriously, but does not take one's self seriously. In doing battle with the Big-Is-Beautiful viewpoint, one needs to avoid being the grim, self-righteous standard-bearer of truth. John V. Taylor speaks of the need for creating a "joyful resistance movement" and organizing a "lighthearted revolution" (*Enough Is Enough,* pp. 68ff.). Such a stance is in tune with the Gospel rather than the Law.

Jesus honored quality of life. His slight rebuke to Martha was that she had missed "the one thing needful." He spoke about a loving Father who was far more concerned about the one lost coin, or the one lost sheep which strayed from the flock than about those many who were complaisantly secure. On the cross he ignored the wagging heads and gleeful dancing of the crowds to center his concern on caring for a brokenhearted mother and a penitent felon.

Can Christians subscribe to the proposition so ingrained into the warp and woof of our society that "bigger is better"? As was mentioned earlier, "growth" is not a big New Testament word. In the one reference that clearly associates growing with grace (2 Peter 3:18), and that seems to be repeatedly quoted by people who are in the curriculum construction business, we are enjoined to "grow in the grace and knowledge *of our Lord and Savior . . . * to *him* be the glory." That statement means that spiritual growth is virtually the opposite of physical growth. There should be more of Christ in my life, and more denial of self, or as John the Baptist put it: "He must increase, but I must decrease." The values of our Lord and those of the scriptural writers do not easily accommodate the current "mindless adulation of growth."

Nowadays consciousness about nonrenewable resources of minerals, chemicals and fossil fuels in addition to the serious pollution of environment is being raised. We are realizing that our inexhaustible appetite for more goods is encountering limits. I was privileged to be in a small group at the first public unveiling of Dennis Meadows' volume, *The Limits to Growth*. He and his colleagues at the Massachusetts Institute of Technology constructed a computerized world-model to show that exponential growth of production can only lead to serious shortages of land and food and to staggering pollution. Those authors knew to some degree the violent reaction their theses would elicit. They also knew a great deal about the shortcomings of the data collected and the difficulties of balancing the factors utilized in their system. Yet, various refinements of their model have only underscored their main conclusions.

Our caretaking of the earth has not been good. The rich nations' greed for ever-greater production is leaving our global village depleted of many necessary resources. Even Garrett Hardin, who made famous the "lifeboat ethic" metaphor, demonstrated that we have a shortage of huge proportions. Christians in facing up to these problems will not alleviate anything by massive "do-gooding" proposals. We will only be a part of the solution if we carefully assess what we can do by means of qualitative alternatives.

Is it impossible to consider small groups of Christians coming together to help one another place an emphasis on quality thinking? We are so absorbed with material values we cannot trust ourselves to do much of a job on our own.

With the paucity of resources available to most Christians, our care taking and care giving must be done prudently. We must begin by assessing our capacities. We might be surprised to find how much we have to offer if we emphasize the qualities of human understanding and expertise in our midst. We need just as carefully to consider where our concern should be directed. I am very excited just now because there is a group of laypersons in our parish ready to embark on a study to see if there is some place in the world where we as a congregation could focus our caretaking most effectively. They are essentially asking: Where can we get the greatest results from our efforts? Possibly there are places where the people are ready to move into something new but need some capital to get started. Then we need to ask where can we invest in something that will multiply efforts many times. These persons are interested in doing something special over and above our other benevolence obligations. Whatever is done, they want to invest in some place where their efforts will stimulate creative response. This is quality thinking.

It is through assessment, evaluation, and establishing priorities that we can emphasize quality care. The American Lutheran Church is launching a program known as Momentum for Mission. Momentum develops when we take time to scrape some barnacles off the hull, divesting ourselves of some pet myths about mission. It will mean inspecting the entire ship to see that it is seaworthy. It will take some careful plotting with navigational devices to perform our mission with a minimum of waste in time and resources. I have seen some of the preliminary measures being taken and am impressed that this kind of care is being invested in this emphasis.

This may mean some radical reordering of priorities in our approach to mission lest the ship of faith get off its course.

But any program of a denomination such as Momentum for Mission must call each congregation to reassess its own program and reorder priorities in this world of rapid change. Do I know where our benevolence monies are going? Do they adequately reflect the changes in our community, nation and world?

Such reevaluation will probably only happen if small groups within a congregation take a new look at their mission. We need not try to save the whole world or our civilization. God will get along without either our world or our civilization. What he asks of us is that we are faithful to the light we have and affirm in some way what he shows us we can do. Small, disciplined groups can accomplish much as can be seen in what happened to the disciples after Pentecost.

Some years ago a Christian student worker was making a mighty splash on the campus of a large public university. He was drawing huge crowds to a Sunday evening program that featured speakers flown in from all over the United States. One day he sat down and asked himself, "What am I really accomplishing with these students?" After much agonizing reappraisal, he decided to purchase a small building near the campus where a few students could be housed, and set up an intense program of Bible study, worship, and small group fellowship. The Sunday evening format was dropped, to be replaced by a new "faith and life community." Every semester a new group of students entered the house and the former occupants were prepared to fan out into the university dorms, there to bring a witness of sharing and caring. He later told me, "I thought I was truly serving Christ with the impressive crowds we were able to attract, but I now know that there is nothing like quality caring." From that campus experiment and through a series of transitions developed the Chicago-based renewal organization known as the Ecumenical Institute, which now extends its quality care experiments all over the world.

# 10

# Caretakers Are Servants

> *. . . who, though he was in the form of God, did not count equality with God a thing to be grasped, but emptied himself, taking the form of a servant. . . .* (Phil. 2:6-7).

At a summer gathering in which the cream of youth leadership from all over the nation were invited, it was suggested by one of the speakers that if someone would throw open a few windows, our stifling hot meeting room might become a bit more bearable. Immediately, four persons got up before anyone else and busied themselves unlatching and winding open the windows. It happened that the four consisted of the denomination's president, a seminary president, and two other officials of the church body, who were present to address or greet this outstanding group of young people. The speaker, whose topic was "Leadership Is Servanthood," could not resist commenting on how this response perfectly illustrated what he was trying to say.

Pope John XXIII did not wish to have all the fancy titles attached to his papal office, such as "Minister of Christ Plenipotentiary" and the like, but asked that only one of these appellations be applied to him. The one he loved and considered quite sufficient was "servant of the servants."

The church at the present moment is not as plagued as it used to be by the old distinctions between "liberal" and "conservative." It is difficult to place persons or movements into one of those categories. Those words just do not apply very well any more. There is a much deeper division today; only it cuts in an entirely different direction. Christians today can be classified as those who hold to a posture of servanthood as opposed to those believing the church is essentially a triumphalistic institution. There are degrees of these stances to be sure. Yet, finally, one must opt for either seeing the church as a group of serving, burden-bearing people, or as that institution in society which can impress others with its pomp and circumstance. The temptation to the latter view is everywhere. When the church wishes to launch a campaign it will often obtain the slickest public relations experts it can find and then proceed to demonstrate to all who will watch that it has as much savvy and money and power as any other institution. To some extent that may be because we are tired of being accused of being naive, poverty-ridden, and unsophisticated. Immigrant church people are especially prone to compensate for their weak and vulnerable appearance.

It is easy to celebrate the resurrection and quietly ignore the cross. There is something exhilarating about presenting the church as robed in rich garments (whether that be an evangelist's $400 suit, or a set of ornate chasubles) triumphantly moving front and center to impress the crowds with its class and supremacy. It is fun to be a winner. It is a good feeling to show success. It is stimulating to be on a victory march.

A profound recognition of how inappropriate such triumphal thinking really is came through that short, plump, "caretaker" pope referred to earlier. He stuck a pin into that pretentious balloon. He called the church back to picking up burdens and getting underneath the cares of others. He reminded us that we belong to the blood, sweat, and agony of Calvary. He told us we cannot be anything finer than servants.

There is a particularly subtle type of triumphalism emerging in church ranks recently. It says if we think positively, the power that is released in us hardly knows any bounds. Often it has an evangelical cast. Its claims are made on the basis of Scripture. The subtle part is the intrusion of ideas mostly from the field of psychology. We might think in this regard of the human potential movements that sweep over the church in different forms about every five years. They stress that we must have a good self-image. We must feel good about ourselves. Now one could hardly argue about that, except that such thinking usurps the keen insight Luther had about persons who know Jesus Christ as being *simul justus et peccator* (at the same time we are justified we are also sinners). It interrupts the rhythm of Law and Gospel in our lives.

Critics of such human potential movements often are portrayed as defeatists, or as not being willing to claim the promises of God. They say God wants us to think "success." After all, doesn't God want for us the abundant life? Now most of these apostles of confidence only hint at the idea that the success that is promised is financial in nature. "Rev. Ike" of TV fames is not so subtle about that. Nor is a certain "foundation" which sends its appeals through the mail claiming that if one contributes to the foundation, one can be sure of financial growth, a healthy life, and blissful happiness in one's family. The basic theme consists of asking one to make a small investment and the dividends will multiply beyond one's wildest dreams. None of these approaches rely upon the need we have for daily renewal through application of Law and Gospel. No, one is told to claim the promises of God continually or one's faith is faulty or possibly lacking altogether.

This word is one people want to hear. There is a steadily growing "electronic church" being formed in our nation. Many of its adherents hold membership in a congregation in their community, but they see no need to participate since their needs are being satisfied by the radio or the tube. The apostles of good cheer are raising billions of dollars a year, and if they can find a way of ministering to people in crisis or work out a system for marrying and burying people, the money will no doubt roll in faster.

This approach seems to see no distinction between the promises of God and those of men. If my hope rests upon the resurrection of Jesus Christ, should that hope insure that I will have a comfortable income, happy children and immunity from untoward tragedies? Was Jesus' life a "success" by these standards? St. Francis of Assisi surely was a fool to give up his good life to become an itinerant beggar. I have trouble identifying even one person with whom I have come in contact and who has been an influence in my Christian life who could claim to be a "success" by these standards.

A faith full of "possibility thinking" is very beguiling. Its message tends to leave us in an aura of inspiration. It blots out much of the misery we all experience in our daily walk. It has tremendous appeal—up to a point. I deal with people on the other side of that understanding of faith oftentimes, if they have not become so bitter as to have given up seeking the counsel of a pastor. It is interesting that people who proclaim some form of equating faith with success have an appeal for just about twenty years. There was a rash of books that came out with these kinds of emphases about that long ago that are now completely forgotten or held in disregard.

Perhaps we should not let this emphasis on equating success with the Gospel trouble us so much. We might better look at the hundreds of congregations not so afflicted. These churches, many of them small and perhaps operating in the open country untouched by media attention, quietly go about serving people in their community and around the world. Not many things that would be considered spectacular happen there but, without being told, the parishioners have a keen sense of what it means to be servants. The dying receive solace, the grieving are surrounded by love and are brought hotdishes, the troubled are invited over for coffee, the local team is celebrated in victory and consoled in defeat, the poor are given clothing and quilts, and some of the offerings go to help the unfortunate half-way around the world that will never be visited. I have spoken in dozens of those churches of late and it confirms my belief that the electronic church could never replace them. God equips them, not with the capacity to be entertained or even to be inspired, but with grace.

Another way of seeing servanthood is through understanding that we need not separate the cross from the resurrection. There *is* pain in the life of the Christian, and to experience such pain is not the result of lack of faith. Indeed, Jesus knew he sent out his disciples as sheep among wolves. Often to be faithful to the Gospel means that we are subject to castigation and rejection. Douglas John Hall in his powerful volume, *Lighten Our Darkness,* calls Christians back to Luther's "theology of the cross," which says we were beggars when Christ found us and we remain beggars all our lives or grace cannot abound. There is no room for a "theology of glory," even in the message of the resurrection. That does not mean we are robbed of joy. The disciples often rejoiced that they could suffer persecution for the faith.

The most powerful visual image Jesus left his disciples took place in that upper room when he got down on his knees to do a task that the most lowly slave refused to do. He concluded that episode by saying: "If I then, your Lord and Teacher, have washed your feet, you also ought to wash one another's feet" (John 13:14).

The clear call to us today is to put away all the tools we use for impressing other people and to take on the posture of servants. This means we will be vulnerable to the taunts of the mighty. It means we must step out and risk being ridiculed and misunderstood. It means we must operate in weakness. There is no other way, especially in a world that places so much confidence in material wealth and making a good impression.

A little volume that helped me see the enormous emphasis the New Testament places on being a servant was *Portraits of a Servant* by John Schultz. It explores many words which unveil the various meanings of servanthood. For example, the word from which we get the English word "deacon" literally referred to waiting on tables, one of the lowliest chores in Jesus' day. For that matter, table waiting is one of those tasks we tip people for today, and one never tips an equal. You remember that the book of Acts describes choosing deacons, one of whom was Stephen, who were to deliver food to the hungry. Another word related to the servant concept was the one we use for "liturgist" today. Originally the liturgist was a person who gave public service similar to that of our civil servants, but later the word applied to a religious and ceremonial specialist who functioned in the temple of Zeus.

Properly understood, the liturgist of today is a servant in the church who represents what worshipers should be in the life of the world. One of the most startling applications of a servant word by New Testament writers was applied to worshipers. The word we translate in Romans 12:1 as our "reasonable worship (or service)" is one taken from the Greek, meaning the lowest of servants. It should remind us that the one who comes to honor and praise God does so in abject humility.

There are other words our English Bible translates "servant." All of them are chosen for their qualities associated with the most menial tasks. The most commonly used word is that which applied to a slave. Some translations use the word slave, but most often we see the concept translated in a more euphemistic way as "servant." Paul uses that word in 1 Corinthians 7:22 when he says: "... he who was free when called, is a slave of Christ." Or again in 2 Corinthians 4:5: "For what we preach is ... Jesus Christ as Lord, with ourselves as your slaves for Jesus' sake." There is not much doubt that Paul's favorite description of Christian living is that we are called to be slaves of Christ. We have freedom only as we are his slaves. We are to enter into relationship with others in such a way as to become their slaves and so to help them live.

What would the church become if it were to be a

servant-church? It would think of itself last. It would continually shade its eyes against the hot sun of oppression to see what help can be given those truly in need. It would find itself repeatedly by losing itself in the wants of others. The radar of the church would be attuned to human need. It would be an organism with long tentacles of care reaching out to surround the wretched of the earth.

This is not just empty rhetoric. There are many congregations and groups of Christians who can be characterized as servants. They do not have the spotlight of the public media trained upon them. To be self-consciously caring defeats what giving care is all about.

Two sons of our congregation have served an inner-city congregation in Chicago. It is a depressing and dangerous place in a city that offers very little hope to many of its residents. Yet to walk into the simple yet beautiful sanctuary, to hear the enthusiastic responses of the people in worship, and to see how the ministry of that congregation brings meaning into the lives of its families is an exhilarating experience. For the pastor, service in that place can be discouraging and disillusioning. Yet the pastor currently serving that parish said to me recently, "I could not think of another of our five thousand congregations that I would rather be serving." It still receives some mission support, and one cannot be in the environment of the church very long without thanking God for having contributed some small part through benevolence dollars to the significant ministry taking place there.

It used to receive more attention and help from more affluent congregations when it was more popular to be concerned about center city ministry. Yet, we seldom hear any words of resentment from its members of what seems to be a diminished interest from the outside. They are too busy multiplying their scanty resources and entering each others' lives with the hope of Christ's love.

If a congregation shall be a serving church, it must begin with each member. We need to ask one another: What would my life be like if I were truly a slave of Christ? A professional football player, the great Gayle Sayers wrote a book titled: *I Am Third.* This man almost immortalized because of his outstanding play with the Chicago Bears adapted his title from the old slogan: "God first, others second; myself last." Am I willing to do the menial, unspectacular tasks in order that God may come first and others next? What would change in my life if I were to clothe myself as a slave? Each of us must answer that question for ourselves.

John Schultz commenting on the opening passage of this chapter says:

> St. Paul is urging us to claim our true humanity. "Have this mind in you," is an invitation to a relationship, a sharing of life with Christ. He is asserting that the relationship of man and God is fulfilled in each taking the form of a servant. God, who is love, is exalted in His slavery to those He loves; man is exalted to true humanness when with Christ he becomes a slave to humanity *(Portraits of a Servant,* p. 31).

Is there any picture one can think of in the New Testament where Jesus does not fully fit the image of being a servant? Wherever we look, even in Revelation, we see him reaching out or lifting up. From him we receive the grace to be his slaves, serving others.

# 11

# To Give and to Receive

*Love [Care] is not arrogant or*
*rude . . . does not insist on its*
*own way . . . does not rejoice in*
*wrong, but rejoices in the right*
(1 Cor. 13:5-6).

We have a delightful lady in her eighties in our
parish whose spirit, energy, good humor, and beauty
make her appear half that age. She travels south with
her husband and other "snowbirds" for a couple of
months a year to escape the Iowa winters. She
spends much of her time in the warmer climes walking in the woods and on the beach to see what she
can spy in driftwood, flowers and leaves and the like.
She gathers these items up and carts them home
with her. Then during the spring and summer she
spends long hours applying her creative and artistic
talents to making things of use and beauty for the
home or children. Just before Thanksgiving, she sets
up a display in her basement of hundreds of clever

and attractive objects her busy hands have fashioned. People from the community and the area stream in by the hundreds to purchase these coveted pieces of art. The considerable proceeds are then donated to a worthy cause, but not just any worthy cause. She has to be convinced this money will be used for someone in real need. After considerable discussion, she chose to give the proceeds of the last couple of years to Lutheran World Relief. She is a Christian giver because she has proper concern for the receiver, those to whom the gift is going. I can think of few examples of caretaking that hearten me more.

Thomas Aquinas expressed the negative side of caring when he said: "It is of the heart of sin that men use what they ought to enjoy, and enjoy what they ought to use." To use something or someone is to make that thing or that person an instrument of our purpose. It is also true that there is so little joy on the earth because our undisciplined lives cannot properly bring into our service that which God placed in our hands to richly enjoy. The world is full of delight and he calls us to revel in it.

Charity can indeed be a problem in the church. Too often we are wont to give in such a way as to attach strings that only tangle up both the giver and the one who receives. Either we want some control over our gift or we desire to manage the persons to whom we give. Perhaps the word "charity" is the problem. It conjures up in our mind someone patronizingly offering a handout to someone less fortunate. When we give, we need to ask: "What is this doing to the one who receives?" At all costs we will want to avoid demeaning another person.

In other words, a gift can really be a gift to ourself, when it gives us a feeling of superior worth. A rich dowager who has her chauffeur drive her down into the ghetto so that she may distribute some Christmas baskets to the poor is giving herself something, but leaving little. That is seeking our own satisfaction through giving.

The Christian giver is not too often "satisfied" in the above sense but is more often than not *fulfilled*. As I write this, I think back on a few events that took place during the past week in the life of our parish. A group of our young people went out to the county home to help with a worship service, to mingle with the residents. They came back glowing from that experience. A family suddenly lost a father and husband and through the ministrations of a colleague were thanking God for the promise of the resurrection at the funeral reception. A small group invited to some members' home to hear from their world-traveling son about *another* cause for a self-help program in India walked out with cheerful and buoyant hearts after subscribing pledges that met the amount needed to get the project started. Arriving in one of the church offices in a distraught condition, a young person, having heard again some great promises from Scripture, leaves with a joyful assurance that he can have confidence that he is a child of God. Several young families having just joined the church gratefully express the thought that their married lives have taken a new and positive turn. What do all of these random instances have in common? Somewhere along the line in those experiences a giver had enabled or strengthened some other person(s) to live more fully human lives. It was the person caring who was fulfilled. Satisfaction may come, as for Shylock, from exacting a pound of flesh from someone else; fulfillment wells up within those persons who can extend a helping hand or nudge other people toward celebrating their humanness in Christ.

We can attempt to gain satisfaction when we give for the direct purpose of controlling others. So many government programs are like that. The Bureau of Indian Affairs has financial resources for those Indians who will do what the BIA says is best for them. A great preponderance of the aid we give other countries is for the purpose of keeping them as military allies. Fortunately, it must be said that at least since 1976 this practice has been changing. For the first time a foreign aid bill separated the military from the humanitarian budget. It went further and insisted that aid first be designated for the very poorest countries, sometimes called the Fourth World. We have also reduced the number of tied loans to poor countries, by which we insisted that they use money lent them to buy our own products. That meant that usually the goods and services cost them twenty percent above the world market costs. We cannot emphasize enough that our policy is changing and that some of the old images of manipulative foreign assistance are receding. Much of that was accomplished through the citizens lobby group for the world's hungry, namely, Bread for the World.

The church can also put recipients in difficult positions. The reason for the legitimate demands from mission fields a few years ago for indigenization was that they became impatient with quietly waiting for additional handouts from the sending churches. Mostly the fears expressed about transition were unfounded. Where indigenous leadership is in charge, some exciting things have occurred in those churches. It also means that the missionary takes on the more difficult but appropriate role of servant.

Can we imagine what a blow to human dignity it is to have to receive charity? I have talked to numerous welfare mothers who describe how they walked around the block several times before boosting their courage enough to go into the welfare office and ask for public assistance. Many others describe how they die a little every time they receive another check. The overwhelming number of people on some kind of government dole are embarrassed and discomfited. It squanders a human being's most precious quality: dignity.

The tragedy is that many Christians believe the above statements about welfare recipients are just not true. Of those I hear saying this, few have talked to anyone on welfare. Let us try to imagine what it would be like if our circumstances suddenly changed and we had no other recourse but to accept help. If we are honest, our imaginations have difficulty stretching that far. Yet we continually hear people cite examples of someone on welfare who is undeserving or possibly cheating.

Giving to others less able to fend for themselves without strings attached does not mean we are irresponsible donors. There is a proper sense in which we should seek accountability. It is the manner in which it is done that is so crucial. For example, if we plan to give to some group, is it better to begin by suggesting what they might do with the aid, or to let them come up with a proposal of their own? The latter is clearly a necessity. Then, on the basis of their own program, the donor should make that group accountable for what happened. That is a far different request for responsibility than prejudicing the situation by saying, in effect: "I know best what you need."

In working with the American Freedom from Hunger Foundation, I reviewed hundreds of proposals from poverty groups in this country as well as overseas. I have never found a situation where the poor did not know best what they needed. It is also true that more often than not the suggestions from those doing the giving would be counterproductive, and in some cases, disastrous. Do we really believe that the people living in the midst of the closed circle of poverty do not know best what they need?

Many of the proposals that came to the foundation I served were from very poor Indian groups. We as a staff were quite often taken aback as we initially reviewed some of these proposals. There would be a plan submitted for a simple gathering place for the young people of the reservation. We would instinctively wonder, knowing how desperate they were for food or a cash crop, why some more practical agricultural program would not make more sense. What we could not see at the time, but later discovered after this building was erected, was that these young people wanted a place where they first could develop their own sense of fellowship and a place where they could better study their ancient roots. Out of that modest building came a number of plans where these young Indians got themselves together and, without outside help, laid out ideas that were later to help their economic situation as well.

Examples from Tanzania come to mind. Several years ago, while the country was still under colonial rule, the British constructed a massive development proposal called "The Groundnut Scheme." The idea was simple enough; it consisted of bulldozing several hectares of verdant jungle and planting peanuts which, it was demonstrated, could grow well in Tanzania. What happened was that when they cleared the ground the hot African sun baked the soil into concrete, and the area was rendered totally unproductive for many years. Now almost any Tanzanian could have predicted this result, but nobody took the trouble to ask a farmer whether this would work or not. Compare that with what Missionary David Simonson is doing through Operation Bootstrap-Tanzania as described in Chapter 2. Simonson calls his school-building program "dignified development." His program takes seriously the pride and worth of the nationals.

The giver must be just as concerned about what his donation does to the recipients. There is considerable documentation now that the great armada of grain ships sent by our government to the Bihar region of India a few years ago actually caused those starving people to give up on several carefully devised development projects. Our Agency for International Development (AID) concluded that that huge operation actually did more long-term damage than good. As sometimes happens, the people develop a dependency syndrome. In the long-term view of things some forms of relief often cause more harm than benefit. It could be reasonably argued that all relief measures, as noble as they might seem, should be abandoned by church agencies in favor of maximizing funds for self-help programs. There is not all that much money available, and we must place it where long-range benefits will accrue. Church aid is only a fraction of what governments can do. Our task should be finding those creative and experimental projects that can be a cutting edge for governmental programs. Lutheran World Relief, for instance, in less than a decade has changed from primarily a relief agency to one that now devotes about eighty-five percent of its funds for self-help development projects.

When I first drove into the city in which I presently reside, Waverly, Iowa, I saw a large sign that read: "Self Help, Inc." Now that word had practically become my middle name as many people know how sold I am on that being the way to go in Christian giving. My inquiries uncovered that an ingenious gentleman in our town by the name of Vern Schield began this operation after going into retirement from a most successful business venture. He had done some traveling in the Third World, going into remote areas and talking with peasant cultivators. It dawned on him that they could utilize a small, maintenance-free tractor. He went home and built such a tractor and his only criterion for donating such a machine is that the recipients be genuinely in need. These tractors are now being shipped to Appalachia, Indian reservations and poorer countries all over the world. This is appropriate technology. Some of these machines have gone a dozen years with little breakdown. People come into our city from poorer areas in this country and from all over the world stating that this is exactly what they need. His eventual dream is to see factories set up in Africa or Latin America to build the tractor wherever it will be used. There is really nothing quite like this diminutive tractor with its attendant plows and discs, though it seems like such a simple idea. Though petrol is in short supply, as Vern says: "It only eats when it works." Oxen do not work that way. Note that he spent many hours talking to destitute farmers to find out what *they* said they needed.

Another great example of a person combining his faith and life with people of another culture is a former missionary, Dr. Carroll Behrhorst, serving in Guatemala. He first came to that land to set up some type of medical mission, but it did not take him long to see that these people needed improved agriculture as much as the skills he could offer them. When the mission board refused his request to help beyond the medical, he organized the Behrhorst Clinic Foundation. Deeply respected by the people because of his concern for them, he has been able to set up a whole host of self-help programs. He has trained scores of paraprofessionals in an intensive two-year study program who now reach far beyond his medical center. His thesis is that we need to help people help themselves, and he has joined Ivan Illich in working out the principles that help people become less dependent on professionals. In addition, Behrhorst has begun self-help programs in farming, education, construction and nutrition. During the Guatemalan earthquake in 1976, a CBS newsman said that he was the one person everyone turned to for leadership. He had earned the people's respect.

Love does not insist on its own way if it knows the sensitivities of the people who are reached out to in love. It is not arrogant and rude, as when people rich in technology move into another culture and demand that people give up their human values. It does not rejoice in injustice and oppression, but seeks to root out the basic causes of hunger and poverty. No matter how painful, love rejoices in the right. It is that kind of perspective on our giving that will cause us to be God's caretakers. The meaning of the admonition in Genesis to "subdue the earth" calls us not to exploit or dominate, but to give it tender, loving care. Then we can better enjoy the means we use to give care.

# 12

# Simple Caring

> *Take no gold, nor silver, nor copper in your belts, no bag for your journey, nor two tunics, nor sandals, nor a staff; for the laborer deserves his food* (Matt. 10:9-10).

Proper caretaking is not all that simple. It would seem to be so much more simple if we could reach into the people's hearts by using the Law, or tell them what God expects of them, instead of relying on the vulnerable message of the Gospel. Caring in a qualitative way means taking time to look deeper into the needs people will in time expose. Caretakers who are truly concerned about the feelings and real needs of those to whom a gift is given desire to know something about the culture, background, and origin of the people they would surround with their care. That takes time and understanding. Is not this all a little too complicated? Perhaps, but is it not more accurate, to say that *we* complicate things? Uninformed caring can often do more harm than good. Simple is not always the opposite of complex as we shall try to show in this chapter.

In the midst of our specialized and cluttered lives, there is one call that makes eminently good sense. It is the call to the simple life. Now voluntary simplicity cannot and should not be defined too precisely. John and Mary Schramm, authors of the excellent volume *Things that Make for Peace,* contend that no one can define what the simple life is for anyone else. There are also a number of ways one can go about establishing an uncluttered life-style which will minimize product consumption and maximize human enchantment. One can do what the Schramms and their family covenanted to do, consciously decide to live in a simple rural setting, growing essential food needs, and cutting frills to the bone.

Another approach that is becoming increasingly popular is to adapt to communal-style living. People in a neighborhood or small community share in buying food in larger lots, trade appliances with one anther, schedule times for the use of common means of transportation, and generally seek to pare away excessive utilization of energy and goods. Other families simply cut away in piecemeal fashion those things not vital to everyday existence. Admittedly, the latter is the most difficult as it requires total family commitment. However, it is reasonable to assume that this is the only option a majority of Christians really have.

What dramatic shrinking there has been in the

size of automobiles Americans are driving these days!
Considering how long and how much of a love affair
the public has had with the large, gas-guzzling machines, this is a most commendable change. One
continues to see an increasing number of homes and
offices turning down the thermostat by a few degrees. Is it my imagination or have I seen an increase
in the consciousness of persons turning off unused
lights or using electricity more sparingly? Many
churches have turned down some convenience-type
gifts simply because they would consume more energy. Many households are not buying added gimmicks, or allowing appliances previously purchased
to fall into disuse. For reasons the networks are
having trouble figuring out, suddenly there was one
million fewer TV sets turned on during prime time.
There are many reasons why people are becoming
conscious of conservation, and opting for a more
simple life-style.

The basic problem with mustering support for
simple living seems to be that many people do not
feel it is necessary. I have spoken with hundreds of
people in recent months who just do not believe, for
instance, that there is an energy shortage. They
speak from several points on the political spectrum.
There are those who say the oil companies are simply
out to scare us so that they may reap enormous prof-
fits. There are others who believe the government
just is not leveling with us. It is unfortunate that
following the OPEC oil embargo in 1973 we tem-
porarily experienced long lines at the gas pumps,
and then suddenly there was a surplus after the price

escalated. Not one person making a serious study of
the energy situation has concluded that we will not
be in real trouble in the next few years. One authority, Amory Lovins, contends that we will have to go
to a decentralized system of providing public power.
Lovins says that we will have to turn back to coal
since solar technology is woefully undeveloped at
present. The breeder reactor could solve some of our
problems but it leaves us vulnerable to extremists or
to careless safety procedures. We have the contra-
dictory situation of the Atomic Energy Commission
being at the same time the agency which promotes
use of atomic plants and also regulates them. Serious
gaps in safety controls have resulted.

It is perhaps irrelevant whether we believe we
have an energy shortage or not. The fact that North
Americans use twice as much energy per person as
the people of Europe, who also have a highly developed economy, should give us pause about our inexcusable waste of nonrenewable resources. Can
Christians allow such carelessness to continue?

What people are discovering is that by stripping
away many of the nonessentials in family life they
find they are rewarded in many ways. Some are
turning to reading again. Many find time to exercise or set out to chop wood for their non-gas or
non-electric powered stoves and fireplaces, shedding
pounds and feeling better. Some come to realize that
an overheated home is not conducive to family activities or good health. E. F. Schumacher reported
that the happiest people he spoke with were those
who had voluntarily chosen to live a more simple

life-style. There is great personal satisfaction in knowing that we do not have to jump into the car every time we must do an errand only blocks away. Walking promotes better hearts, stronger limbs, and clearer heads. Dr. Fredrik Schiotz, President Emeritus of the American Lutheran Church, and Mrs. Schiotz plan their day so as to include a brisk two mile walk. The results show in their undiminished zest for life.

Many seem resigned to saying that we will not get down to the business of conservation or simplifying our life-styles until we are forced by necessity to do so. Yet we want to bequeath to our children and grandchildren the benefits of our social, economic and political system. Why are we so resistive to cutting back on our life-style? We are only two generations away from an economy of scarcity. Surely many remember the quaint way in which grandparents saved string and every single usable item almost as a matter of reflex. If they lived that way, why should we find it so difficult at least to try to move in that direction?

Much of the squandering of energy or even of food can be laid to one basic cause: *convenience*. We have a passion for conveniently processed and packaged foods as well as for those gadgets and gimmicks that make our life easier. Do they make life easier? A colleague of mine, Pastor Glen Wheeler, wrote a statement on this problem that we might title, "Confessions of an Energy Addict":

> • In a period of reflection with other members of this congregation, I discovered some horrifying

things about myself and my chosen life-style. When I examined my own value system in the use and abuse of energy resources the one common denominator was the *desire for convenience.*

I suppose I could say like a user of hard drugs that I started innocently enough—with just a simple desire to have things as convenient as possible. That seems like a harmless beginning, and yet the desire for personal comfort and convenience has grown into an unbreakable habit.

With careless disregard for the consequences to my children and my grandchildren, and to air, soil, water and nonrenewable energy:

• I want my bath water hot not only when I need it, but also for the other twenty-four hours of the day.

• I want my drinks cold at all times with easy opening nonreturnable containers.

• I want my home to be a comfy seventy degrees on both the coldest day and the hottest day of the year.

• I will spend thirty to forty percent of my income and burn up gasoline stolen from my grandchildren so that I can have instantaneous private transport to any place of my choosing for the sake of my convenience, rather than support public means of transporting people which would also include elderly and children.

• I will have my meals packaged conveniently and individually in tons of nonreturnable packaging.

• I will have all my rooms brightly lighted and be served by an unending array of electrical gadgets which I have been persuaded I could not possibly live without, yet most of which were unknown a few decades ago.

But most horrifying of all, this convicted energy
addict has serious doubts whether he or the culture
which has enslaved him has any intention of re-
penting and renouncing this idolatry committed at
the altars of convenience. It is hard to rehabilitate
a person or a society that has fallen in love with
its chains.

It is not a part of God's economy that many should
endure a hand-to-mouth existence while others live
in wasteful opulence. He provides all that the people
of this globe need for daily essentials. The problem
is not that his cornucopia is even close to being bare.
The problem is distribution, and that is a man-made
situation that can be changed. But there must be
some spilling over of holy discontent. The community of Christ must help others to strip away the
unessentials of comfort and convenience.

The strange truth of the matter is that we do not
sustain a more simple life-style by grimly resolving
to endure the austere life to the bitter end. It is
much like trying proportionate giving. The more we
try it, the more we like it. To take a leap into the
quieter, less complicated style of life is similar to
coming out of a sauna bath. It may look forbidding,
but there is nothing so relaxing and releasing.

The simple life, to use the phrase of an oft-repeat-
ed advertisement, is "curiously refreshing." Voluntary simplicity "uncomplicates things." One needs to
go no further than the earthly life of our Lord to
realize that our slavish attachment to things is not
what God had in mind when he placed us here.

Another reason for our unquenchable thirst for

activity and movement and for goods and services is that there are so many opportunities. Like children in a candy store, we are bemuddled by the over-abundance of all that is so appealing around us. Having too many choices means we must set up priorities. One management consultant says that an executive should place his paperwork in three piles. "Place the most important materials in the center of the desk; that which is of middling priority should be put away for another day. The last pile should be placed in a drawer and should be forever ignored." Without priorities, only the urgent becomes necessary.

Yes, opportunity abounds. This includes worthwhile things like concerts to attend, mini-courses to take, colleges in which to enroll in midyears, and a multitude of places that cry for volunteer workers. We need to sit down every so often and examine the opportunities in our community and take advantage of these varied resources.

Shopping centers are becoming massive temples that draw hordes of worshipers at all hours. Within them, specialty shops multiply and divide like cells. The only opportunity some families take for being together is a jaunt to the nearest shopping complex. The kids can be outfitted for school. Mom can enjoy the enticing things in store windows. Dad can bring home a cheese or nut specialty for munching during the late night TV show. This uses gas. It also consumes spare money in the wallet. Instead of the blessings of "enjoy, enjoy," our motto becomes "consume, consume." One of our local car merchants ends his sales pitch with the word, "buy!" He is not bidding us farewell.

To cut away that which is unessential in our lives will call us to take a closer look at the Gospel. From what has Christ freed us? He has freed us from ostentation and conspicuous consumption. He has freed us from an unmanageable appetite for fun and games. He freed us for a life of quiet service and for knowing the deep satisfaction that overwhelms us in enjoying him forever. When Jesus sent out his disciples they went with no spare money, bag, tunic, or sandals. He did not want them unnecessarily encumbered for their mission. They were stripped for action.

Where do we begin to make our care style more spare? We begin by confessing our consumer addiction. We begin by talking about this as a family where often the young have keen insight. We begin by speaking about this in small groups within our parishes. We continue by making our simplified care style a "light-hearted revolution" to use the phrase from John Taylor. God wants us equipped sparingly for our daily mission because he knows that is the only way to go.

No call has come to the American church with greater clarity than that which addresses us now. The church was called in the past to give our nation a sense of direction. It continued to be called westward as a part of our "manifest destiny." It has been called more recently to abandon its flight to the suburbs and to minister to the city. Now it is being called to face the great fact of our time—the division of the world between the rich and the poor. Surely if we cannot strip down our own life-style that we may provide better for the great masses of the poor, can we honestly believe God will continue to bless the American church?

Christians care. There are many ways of demonstrating that care. One of the most promising ways is in the stripped-down life-style. To live in a simple, uncluttered fashion brings rich rewards. Perhaps the most notable is found in the results of being better stewards of our bodies. At the same time we are preparing the young for the day when many resources will be in shorter supply than they appear to be now. Conservation is the very heart of a Christian's care style. When we add these benefits to the possibility that we may be more generous toward the economically depressed of the world, we will gladly join in a few choruses of the popular ballad: "Give me the simple life!"

# 13

# The Consummate Caretaker

*He is before all things, and in
him all things hold together. He
is the head of the body, the
church; he is the beginning, the
first-born from the dead, that in
everything he might be pre-
eminent. . . . I rejoice in my
sufferings for your sake, and in
my flesh I complete what is
lacking in Christ's afflictions for
the sake of his body, that is,
the church . . .* (Col. 1:17-18, 24)

I once had this dream. I dreamt that Jesus came
to our congregation and applied for a job. I thought
I knew who he was, but I was not entirely sure.
I remember panicking, and the insistent question
that came to my mind was: If he is who I think he
is, what position would he want? The question never
was: What position would he take? That would be
the ultimate in presumption. Would he want to meet

deadlines, counsel marriage partners, go to meetings, make birthday calls, teach confirmation, plan with the youth, give private communions, visit the sick, or preach and teach? I began to realize, as I thought about that, how he would change the priorities of the pastoral job. I remember feeling shamed. There is no position in our church, paid or unpaid, that he would not fill because he would be continuously touching people's lives in whatever capacity he would act. And it came to me in a flash. It seemed suddenly very fitting and appropriate. He would slip on a pair of denims and a work shirt and head over to our broom closet. He would want to go down into our boiler room and find out what carpenter tools we had. It struck me as a vivid reality. This is what he would want, and this is the job for which he would apply. It did not make any difference when I thought again that our present custodian is an attractive young woman. He would simply step right in and work along with her as her much-needed assistant. The dream was never completed, but I remember recalling it when I awoke, and it all seemed very apropos.

We Christians claim a convicted criminal as our King. We worship as Lord one who stands among us as a slave. We call him Savior whose flesh was stretched helplessly across two planks of wood in his saving act. We say that this itinerant teacher who walked about with his rag-tag disciples is the fulfillment of all the hopes and dreams of Israel. We speak of this man who felt comfortable with the most depraved and degenerate of human beings as the one who brings us into the messianic age. To him who was passionately hated by the most religious and pious people who were his contemporaries, we give titles like "Son of God" and "Son of man." He is the Consummate Caretaker.

I grew up on the campus of Concordia College in Moorhead, Minnesota. From my early boyhood, until the time I enrolled in that institution, I knew scores of distinguished teachers and effective administrators. Two people left an indelible imprint upon me. One was Nels Mugaas, a single man, stunted in stature, who seemed to be omnipresent on that campus. Many nights, as a small boy, I followed him around as he locked up the buildings. He would invite me into his dorm room, and there was hardly a time that a student did not come in to talk to Nels about something. Later, when I was a bit older, I learned that he had made several loans to students, especially during the depression years. I forced it out of him one evening on a visit back on Navy furlough, and he told me about people successfully working in their chosen field whom he had helped when they could not scare up another nickel. Many paid him back and many did not. He must have, on his pitifully low salary, loaned thousands of dollars to struggling students. Nels was a caretaker.

The other person I remember well was Hegland Grundfer. Everybody called him by his last name, without the "mister." He was found most often down in the boiler room. I do not remember him smiling much, and his speech was gruff and unpolished. He was always covered from head to toe with soot and grease. There was not anything he could not repair. Many referred to him as a mechanical genius. But he was so much more. He loved to sit in the boiler room and tell the neighborhood kids, my peers and me, stories about Peter Rabbit. They always had more theology in them than my Sunday school classes did. The students recognized him as a philosopher; so when kids were not around, he would wax eloquent on a number of subjects with the former students. There were those who poked fun at him, which I could never understand as I almost never remembered his gruffness nor the grease but the fact that he took time with people. He looked no different to me on Sunday mornings when I saw him in church scrubbed and wearing a threadbare black suit. I later learned many more things about how he and his wife reared children who were without parents, since they had only one child of their own. One of those foster children was to become the head of the philosophy department of that college and one of the brightest young men I know. Grundfer knew how to care.

Jesus is like that famous scrub lady whom Luther described as one who polished the stone floors so that they shone; thus she gave service to her fellows, and fulfilled her God-given calling. He lived and worked, preached and taught in a tiny land, but he is able to escalate the consciousness of the most provincial among us and widen the horizons of the narrowest dullards we know. He continually, after all, does it with me. He taught by means of stories that had to do with the most common and ordinary experiences of the lives of those with whom he spoke, and thereby pointed them, and us, to the mysteries of heaven. He chose the common elements of the earth to signify the holy. He does not permit us to separate the ordinary from the spiritual. This Caretaker addresses us by name, and in that singularly personal experience, joins us together with a family that extends to the uttermost parts of this globe. Jesus unlocks the prison of our own society and its value system as he unlocks other cultures to enrich our lives together. This humble carpenter's son is declared to be the Lord of all of life. He did not have a place to lay his head, and he still wanders alone through the earth to invite us into his mansions of glory. He is the Consummate Caretaker.

Now, what shall we do with this Caretaker who presents himself to us in his overalls and with his carpenter tools in hand? We shall not manage him. We shall not fit him into our scheme of values. We shall not be able to put on a mask to deceive him. We shall not be able to impress him, not even with the most beautiful prayers ever written or strings of merit badges that hang down to our knees. He defies all this.

What shall we do with him? We shall worship him. We shall praise him in our kitchen, our office, or in the privacy of a prayer chamber. We shall kneel at the altar and accept a bit of bread and a glass of wine and utter a quiet "thank you." We shall come together at the funeral of a friend and sing with a loud voice about our eternal destiny. We shall pour out our needs, our dependencies, our ineptitudes, our weaknesses and, yes, our ugliest sins, gathering them all up in our arms, and placing them before his cross.

I have just conducted the funeral service for Fred who in many ways came the closest to being a Jesus figure in our community. He lived alone in a trailer outside of town. He had not one close friend. People often described him as the most thoroughly broken and helpless human being they had ever known. But they did not know him very well. He could barely talk with one without weeping; such was his emotional state most of the time. He did not cook decently for himself and could not manage his finances very well. We spent many hours together when he seemed downhearted, which was often. I tried to help him buy the right foods from the puzzling diet his doctor gave him. I took him quite often to doctors and hospitals and sought to settle the bills. He could not be helped much by his family as most were scattered, and it was hard to know where to begin to help. If he was more broken and helpless than most, he knew his condition better than the rest of us. All week, people have been telling me of one thing after another that he did for them as an unexpected service. Many of the jobs around the church that no one else wanted to do, he undertook. And, oh, did he understand the grace of God! He loved to have someone share the Scriptures with him, especially those treasured promises that tell us God cares. When one would underscore again that Jesus cared for him, his face would twist into a hard-wrought smile, abruptly he would get up, offer a quiet word of thanks, and limp off unsteadily. For the last several weeks I had been trying to get him into an old folks home. Now he is in a home for new folks.

Caretakers are not born; they are made—made by the one who reaches down to the most helpless among us and enfolds that person in his love. We cannot grit our teeth and resolve to be good caretakers for God. We cannot force ourselves into being tithers. We cannot force-feed our concern and thereby feel sorry for the millions of people who do not have one-fiftieth of what we use and possess. When we see how much care we need and how much care Jesus offers, then maybe we can become caretakers to others.

Of all the people who have sought to bring renewal into the American church in the last couple of decades, Clarence Jordan of Americus, Georgia, strikes me as being the most authentic. He lived and died to form a little community which set up all kinds of self-help programs for the poor. He suffered many personal indignities because of his friendship with black people. His "cotton patch" translations are known around the world. He had some radical notions of what it means to be Christ's caretaker. Bill Lane Doulos, after Jordan's death, put together some of his views on the parables in a little paperback titled *Cotton Patch Parables of Liberation*. In that volume, Doulos (yes, that is the original Greek word for slave) tries to show how explosive the stories Jesus told really are.

> When we attempt to fit our Christianity into our culture, we are really attempting to fit a square peg into a round hole. We are trying to mix oil and

water. Or we are trying to put new wine into old
wineskins. The parables that say best what we must
do when we encounter the kingdom—either by accident or after years of searching—are the twin parables found in Matthew 13:44-46. . . . Clarence
put it like this: "The kingdom of God is like a man
plowing in a field. He discovers a treasure, a box.
He's plowing his old ox there. All of a sudden he
hits something, and he thinks it's a rock or a stump,
and yet he sees it glitter like metal, and he quickly
throws his plow aside. He scratches around and
finds it is a treasure box.

"What does he do? Well, he might say, 'You
know, this is a very wonderful discovery I've got.
I think I will go to school and write a Ph.D. disser-
tation on treasure-hunting.' But this isn't what he
does. In his great excitement, this guy has the ability to decide on a clear-cut decisive course of action. He says, 'I'm goin' to sell *all* I've got and buy
that field.'

"He's got a sign up in the classified ads, For Sale:
one house; For Sale: one fiberglass boat; For Sale:
this and that. He is goin' out of business. But is he?
He's just gettin' ready to go *into* business. This man
knows what he's doin'.

"I think a lot of times we don't go into the kingdom business because we just aren't smart businessmen. We want to hold on to our little trinkets.
We want to hold on to our status. Oh yeah, we
gotta keep our status. We can't be fools for Christ.
We can't give up our house. So this guy is ready to
sell out in order to get this treasure of great price.
This is the kingdom; this is part of the revolution.
And in order to be in the revolution you many
times have to divest yourself of all earthly possessions. You gotta make some adjustments in your
standard of living. And the adjustments that Jesus

generally calls on people to make are not adjustments upwards but adjustments downward" (pp.
17-19).

"Adjustments downward" are what we have been
appealing to in this volume. We want to take care.
We want to be some of Christ's foolish caretakers.
We will not be able to duplicate Jesus' methods.
Let us take a good look at this Consummate Caretaker. Let us worship him. We must look at this
Jesus in contrast to a triumphal church that seeks to
go around impressing people. We must be done with
thinking that faith has something to do with "success." We must adjust that life-style downward to
less unseemly proportions and allow human feelings
to flood our spirit. We dare not let the starving out
of our sight. We must take time to look over our
human foibles. We are going to say: "I'm not OK,
and you're not OK; but with God, *that's* OK." And
we will see Good News pouring out of the heart of
the great Caretaker.

Meanwhile, how shall we say it? . . . *take care.*